The Lake District: Paintings

Peter Symonds

Published by Northern Arts Publications
an imprint of Jeremy Mills Publishing Limited
www.jeremymillspublishing.co.uk

113 Lidget Street
Lindley, Huddersfield
West Yorkshire HD3 3JR

First published 2012

ISBN: 978-1-906600-76-1

Front cover: *Bright Beck and Stickle Tarn*
© Peter Symonds

Acknowledgements

My special thanks to my wife Vanessa for her constant support, understanding and keen eye in her critique of my work. Also to Clive for translating my scrawl and typing out the script. Finally my thanks go to Des, Niki and Karen at Beckstones for their professionalism and encouragement over the fourteen years that they have been promoting and selling my paintings of the Lake District.

Foreword

'Absolutely breathtaking' – this is a reaction we have heard over and over again from visitors when faced with a Peter Symonds original for the first time. Peter is considered by many experts, art critics and fellow artists to be one of the truly elite artists of his time and can be justifiably described as world class.

Peter has had a lifelong love affair with the Lake District, and although he occasionally paints other locations, his true and enduring passion is the Lakes. Bright sunshine or partial shade on the Lakeland fells, water shimmering in the sunlight, misty valleys or bright blue skies are all used to dramatic effect. Peter's work moves beyond mere topographical accuracy and his fluid, exquisite brushwork together with his use of tone and light bring the finished painting to life. Although one experiences the impression of intricate detail, closer inspection reveals that this is something of an illusion, such detail being conveyed with the minimum of fuss, always finely observed and perfectly lit, but never overworked.

It has been a great pleasure to work closely with Peter over the last fourteen years and we look forward to our continued association with this extraordinarily talented painter.

Niki Langley   *Karen Tennant*
Beckstones Art Gallery

The Western Shore, Crummock Water

It is very easy to run out of superlatives while writing or talking about the Lake District. It wouldn't be difficult to describe countless places as the most ideal location but if I was forced to make one choice for my perfect setting, this has to be it. At the foot of Crummock Water there is a long shingle beach where we love to go as a family. A few hundred metres up the lake from here is the view portrayed in this painting and I have never seen it look as majestic as it did on this day. My wife would have been glad I was on my own as otherwise she would have been bombarded by my eulogising of how utterly breathtaking it was. 'Yes Pete, it is, but we've heard it all before!' This, however, was a day for superlatives, and the light catching the snow on Great Gable in the far distance was the proverbial 'icing on the cake'.

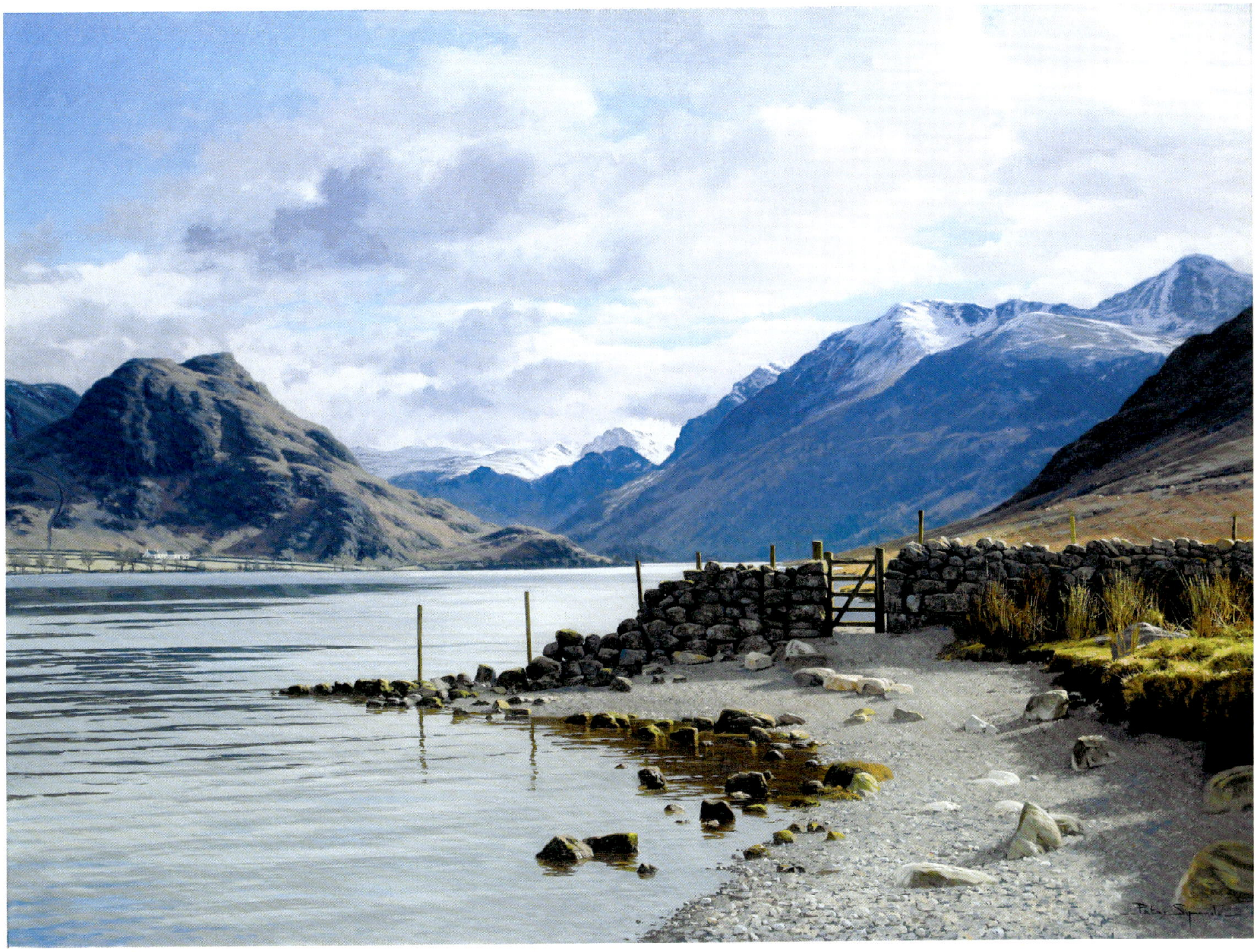

Moody Sky, Stickle Tarn

The usual approach to Stickle Tarn is from the New Dungeon Ghyll Hotel in Great Langdale, but on this occasion I came over from the north-east via Easedale Tarn. Heavy, rain-laden skies promised another soaking, but as I reached for the waterproofs, the clouds parted and flooded the foreground in a wonderful light. Shortly afterwards, the sun lit up the bulk of Harrison Stickle behind the tarn, but I felt it would make a far more pleasing picture by keeping the hill in shadow. The whole effect only lasted for a few minutes, but I felt I had seen the tarn and fells look at their most dramatic. A little later, Harrison Stickle disappeared into the clouds and I was left needing the waterproofs!

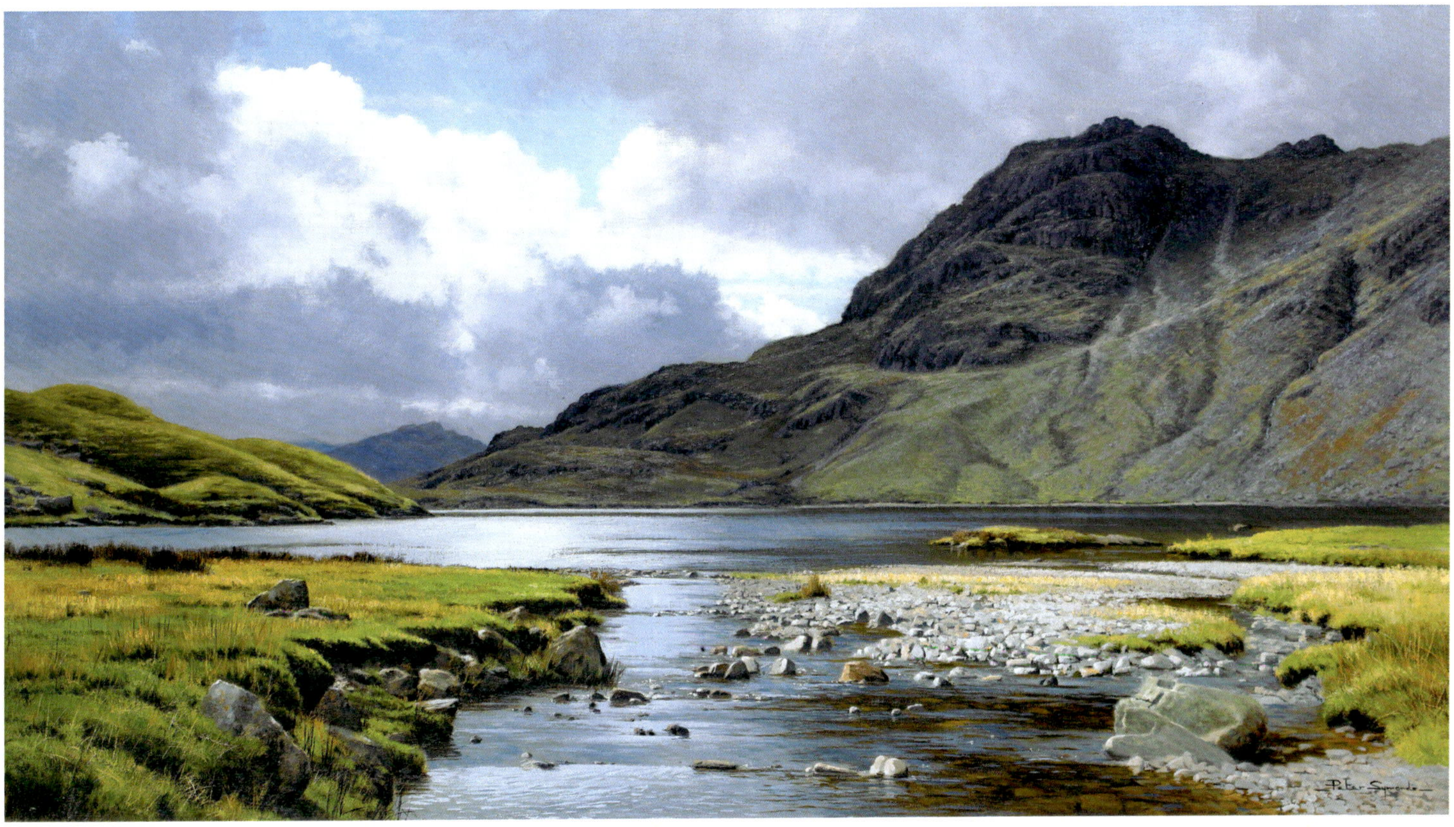

Mellbreak and Crummock Water

This is surely one of Lakeland's finest lowland panoramas. There is a great sense of space when one stands before this view. In order to include all the well known distant fells in the picture, I decided to use a long horizontal canvas at the expense of putting too much emphasis on the sky.

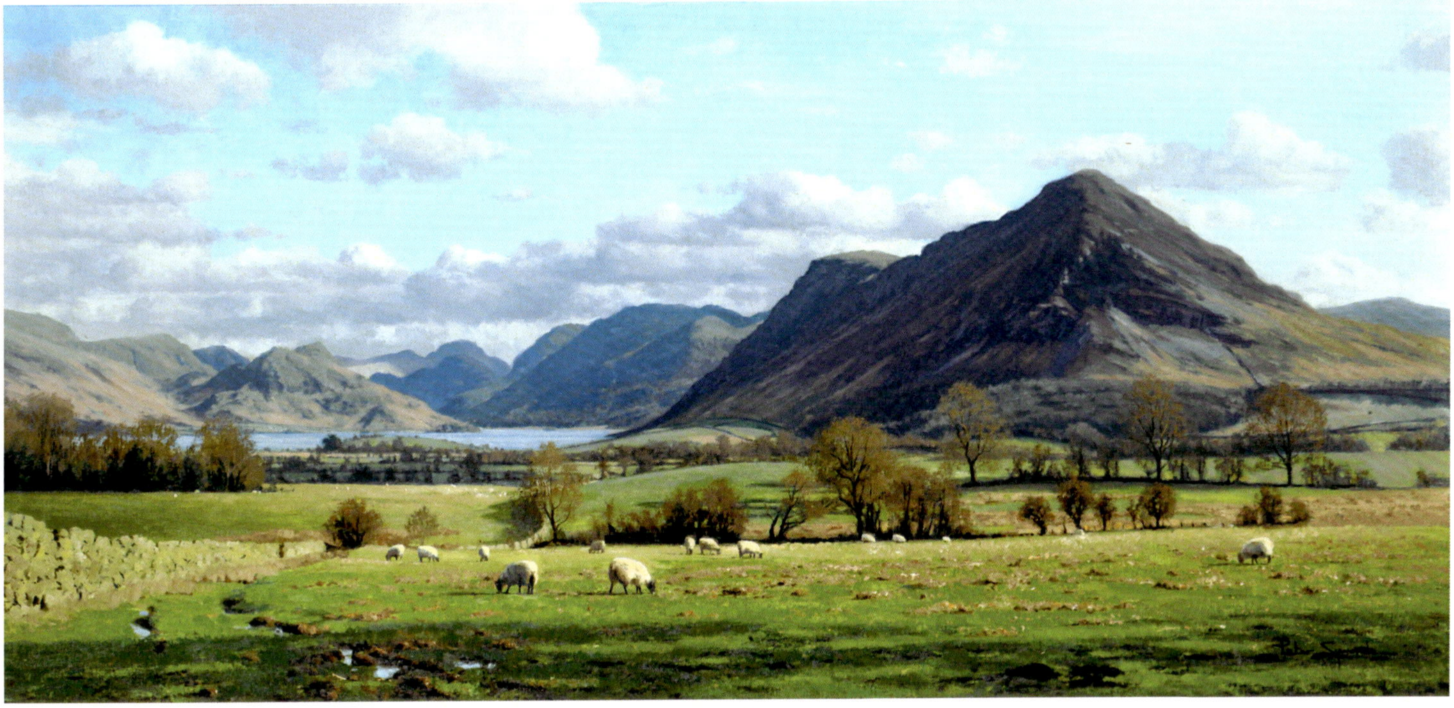

Late Afternoon, Mickleden, Great Langdale

This is the majestic vista that is familiar to all who descend into Great Langdale on the steep twisting road from Blea Tarn. Many people stop and photograph the view from further up the hill, but I think it makes a more appealing composition with the road and the beck in the foreground, leading the viewer's eye along to the focal point of the tree and barn.

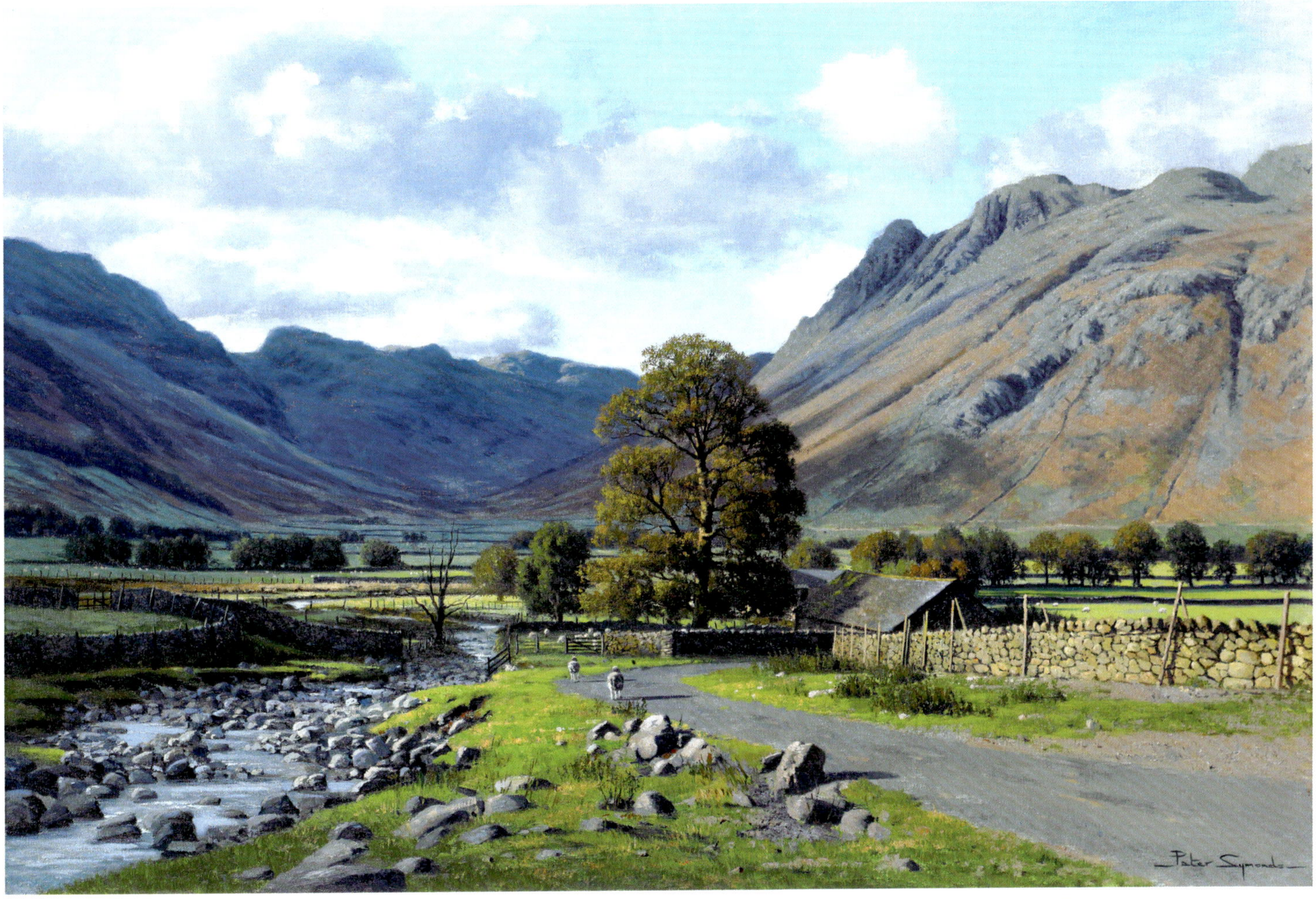
Peter Symonds

Blea Tarn House

Epitomised in Wordsworth's poem 'The Solitary', this delightful scene can be found a short way down the road from Blea Tarn on the way to Great Langdale. I originally painted this view in 1992 and it was the first of my paintings to be published as a fine art print. It was reprinted on quite a few occasions, but is no longer available. A man bought a copy of this print many years ago in Ambleside. Having taken it along to the actual location he then returned to the gallery, a little upset that the artist had not portrayed the scene accurately. Apparently, I had left a couple of hanging baskets and a window pot out of the painting!

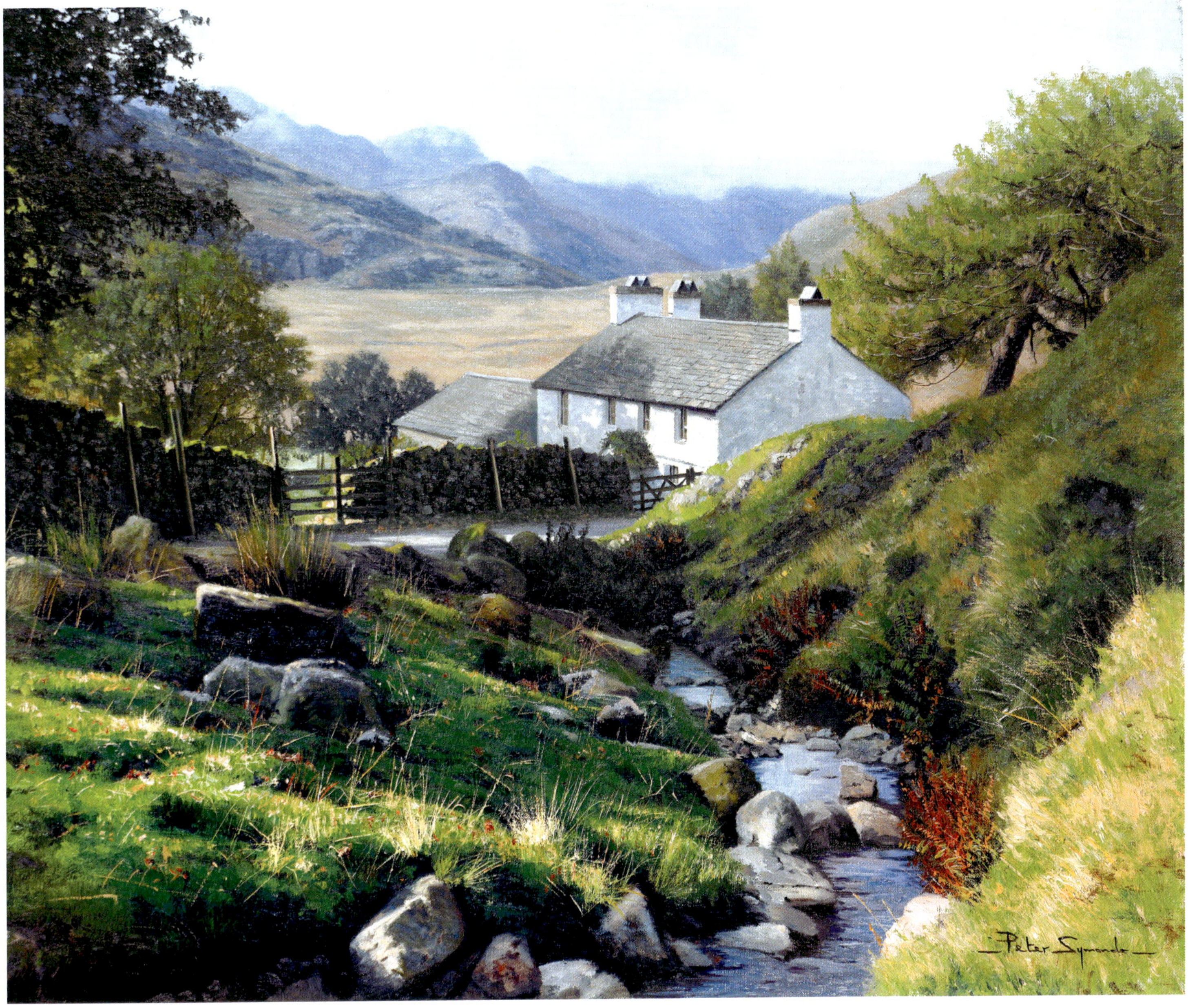
Peter Symonds

May in the Langstrath Valley

On several occasions I have set off from Stonethwaite on backpacking trips with friends. The excitement of what lies ahead always starts to materialise when the first uninterrupted view of the Langstrath opens up. I rarely paint the Lake District during the summer months as I find the carpet of greenery from valley floor to fell top rather monotonous. This was one of the exceptions to my rule as I feel the trees here look rather better when in leaf. This is my favourite river walk in the Lakes and I can thoroughly recommend it to anyone who has yet to do it.

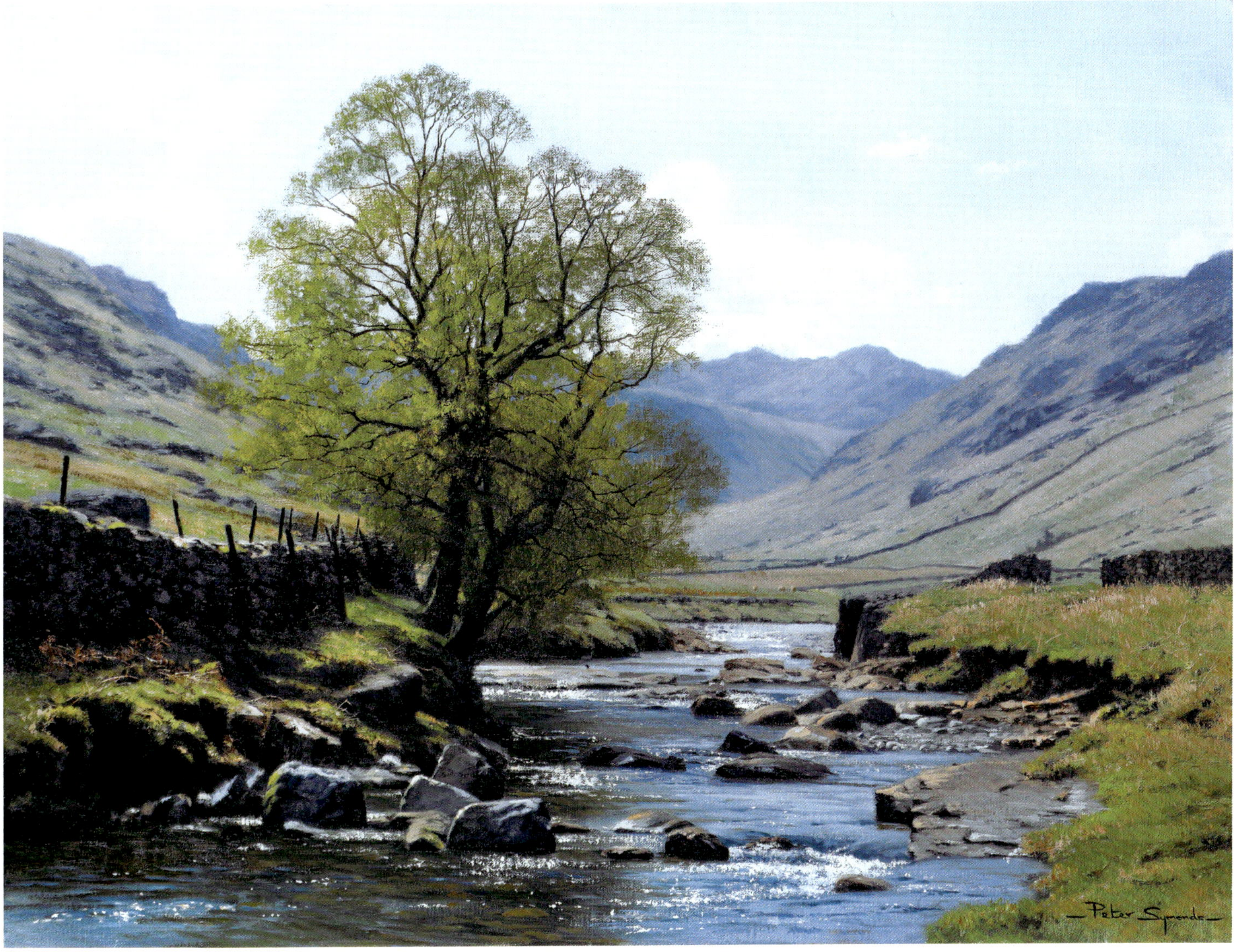
Peter Symonds

Early Morning, River Duddon, Cockley Beck

The effort of waking early and being in the right place at the right time when the rising sun first lights up the landscape often proves worthwhile. One has to start even earlier when Cockley Beck is the destination as it is a remote place midway between the Wrynose and Hardknott Passes. As is so often the case in the Lakes, little artistic licence was needed for this subject – it is a gift of a scene to paint.

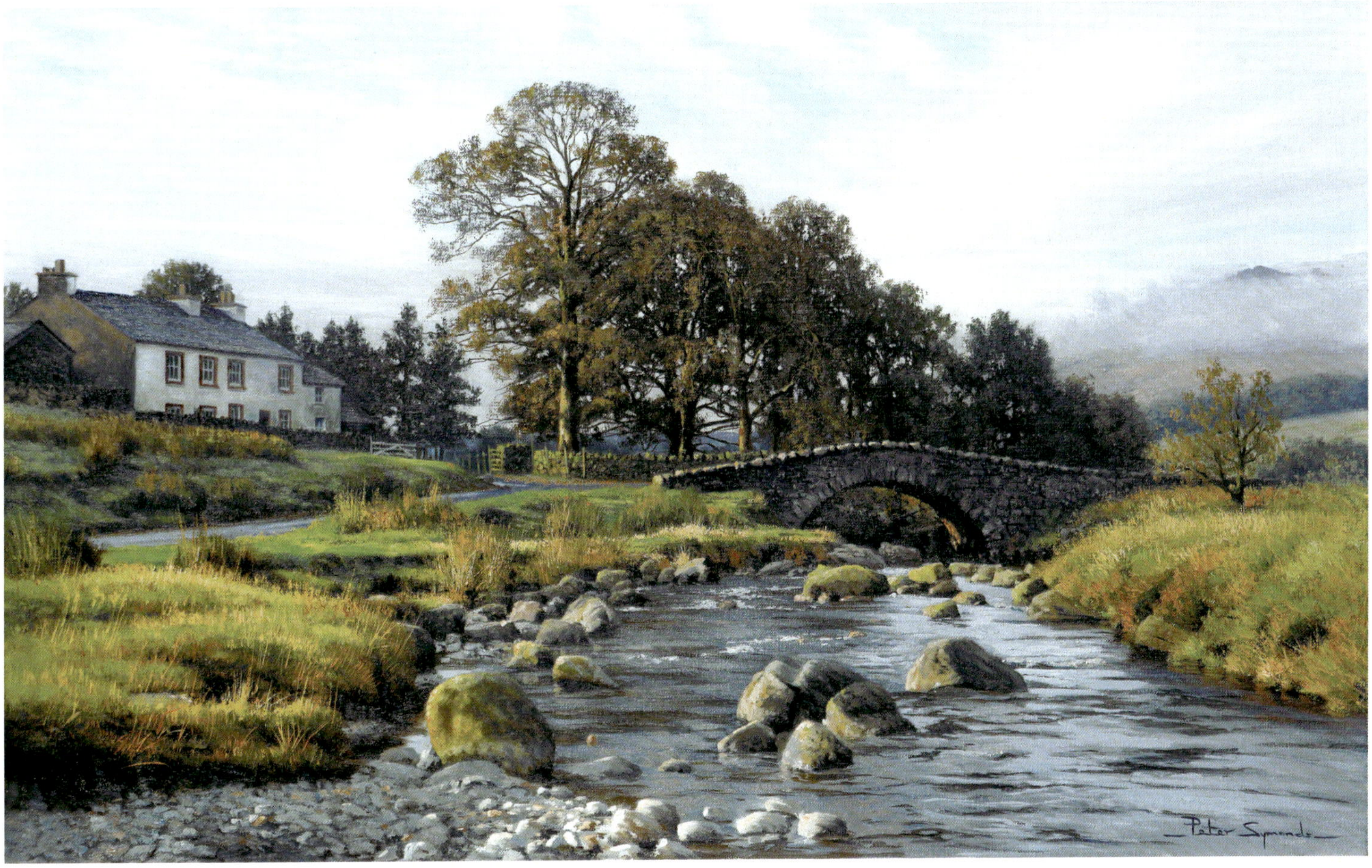
Peter Symonds

Dawn, Friar's Crag, Derwentwater

This has to be one of the most famous views in the Lake District. For that reason, until recently, I have resisted competing with the endless paintings and photographs of this much frequented spot. On this occasion, however, I was sidetracked from another scene I was going to paint by the warmth of the rising sun catching the trees and bank on the right of the picture. It was a very cold morning and the ice on the foreshore easily took my weight.

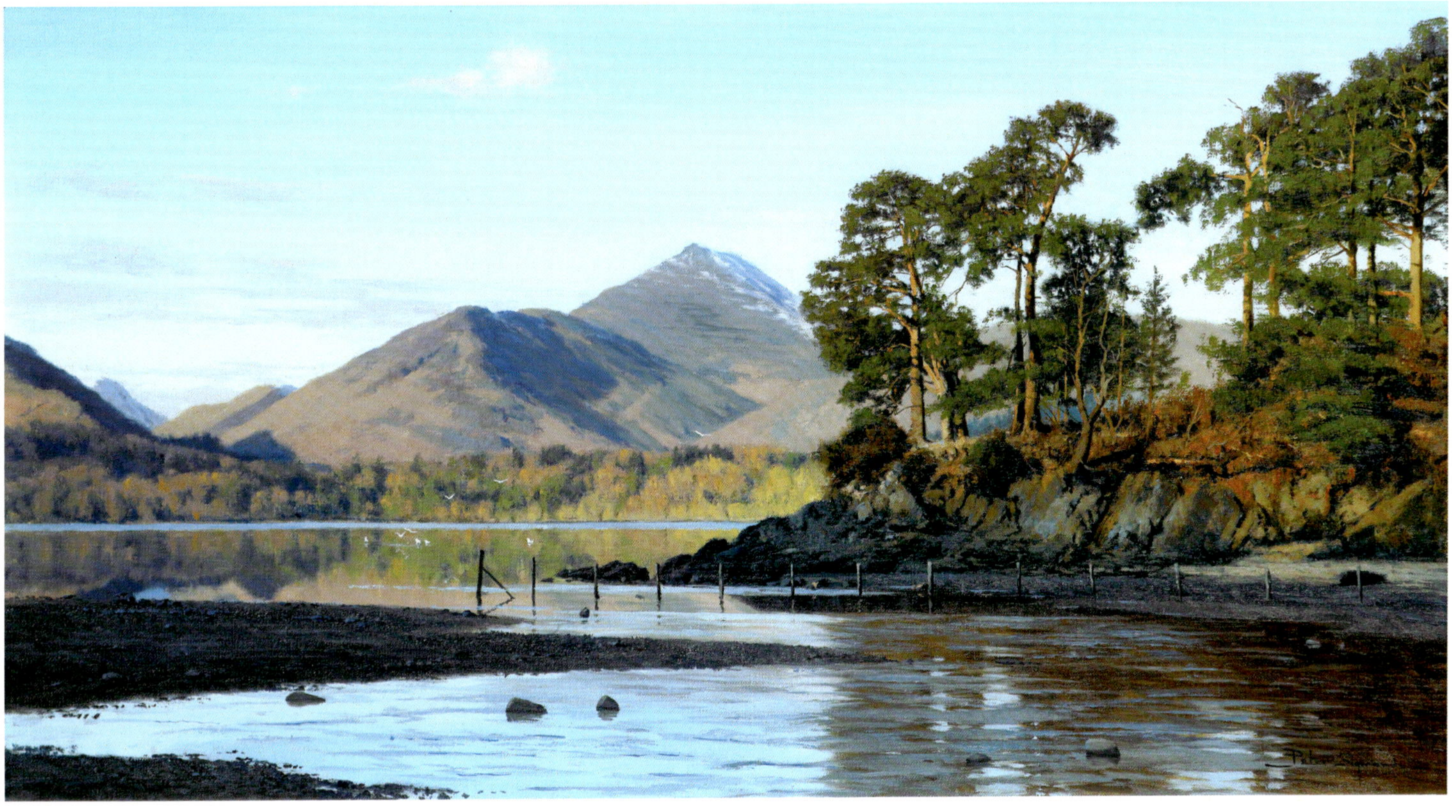

Scots Pines, Glenridding Beck

I love to paint water and a high proportion of my work includes it somewhere. Painting rocks and boulders in fast flowing streams has been one of my greatest challenges, and it took nearly four days to paint the foreground of this painting.

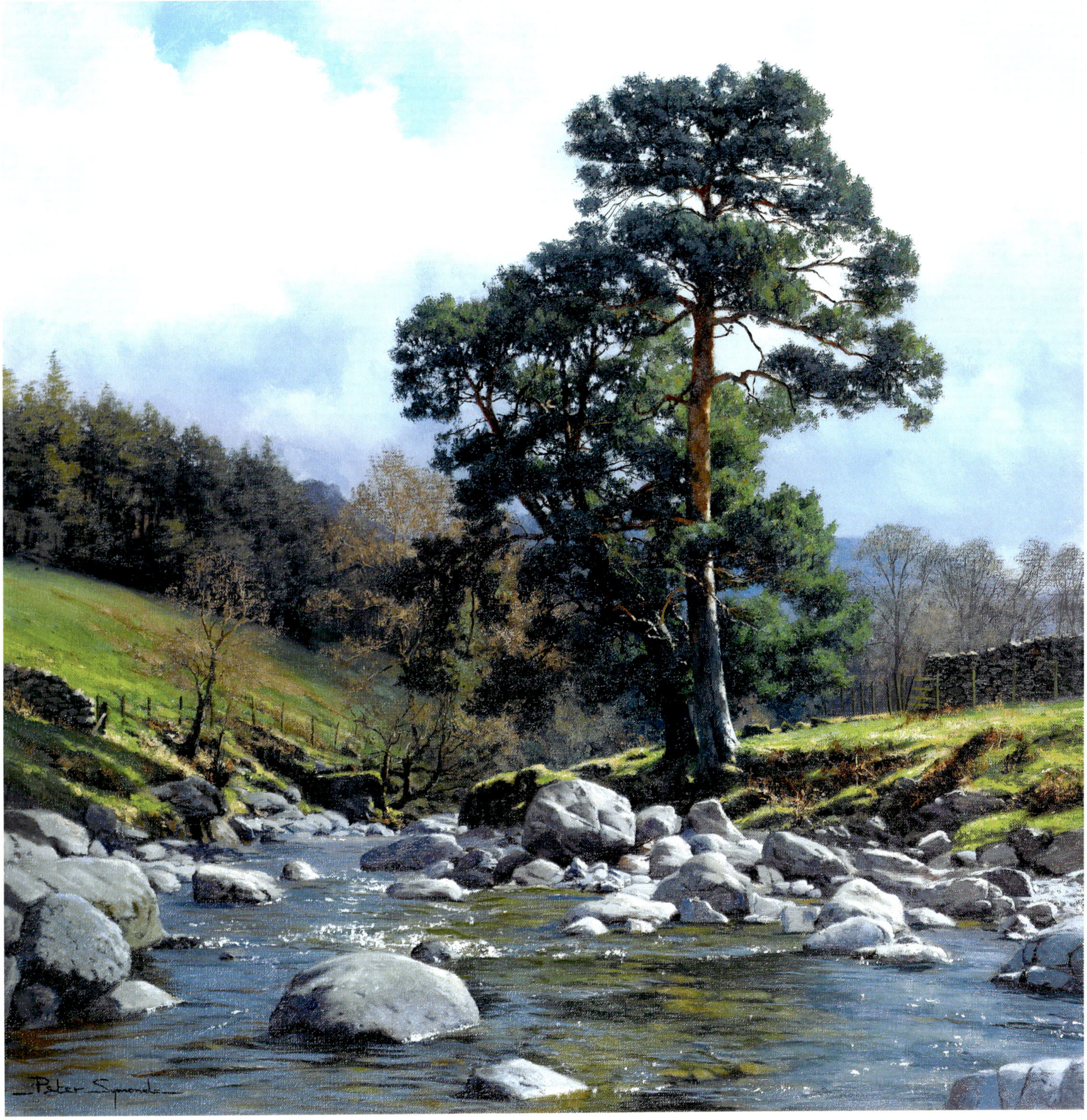

Day's End, Mellbreak from Buttermere Dubs

The final hours of the day as the sun steadily descends towards the horizon is a lovely time. The sunlit areas of the landscape pick up a warm hue, while the shadows turn bluer as seen here on Mellbreak's flanks. By keeping the foreground grass in shadow, I was able to focus the eye on the golden reeds in the centre of the painting at the place they meet the cool tones of the fell above.

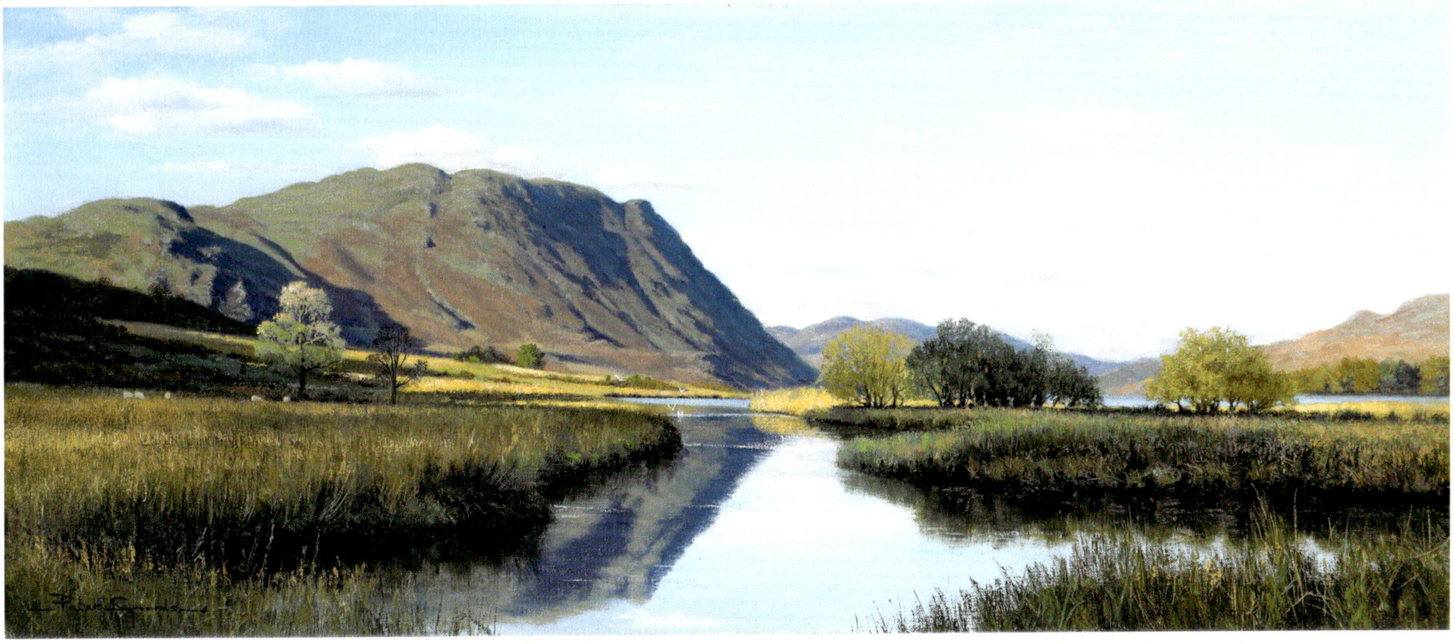

The Way Home, Deepdale

The weather forecaster's promise of a fine day looked a bit optimistic as an ominous bank of clouds hung forlornly over the fells. Luckily it didn't take long for some of the clouds to lift, and much of the valley was bathed in a beautiful light. The scene was everything a landscape artist looks for, but it was the atmospheric conditions that gave it that edge. I felt really blessed to see the dale look like this, as it makes for a far more interesting picture with the blue shadows on the fells contrasting nicely with the grasses in the foreground. On several occasions, the sun lit up the trees in the middle distance, but the scene was far more exciting and powerful when they were kept in shadow.

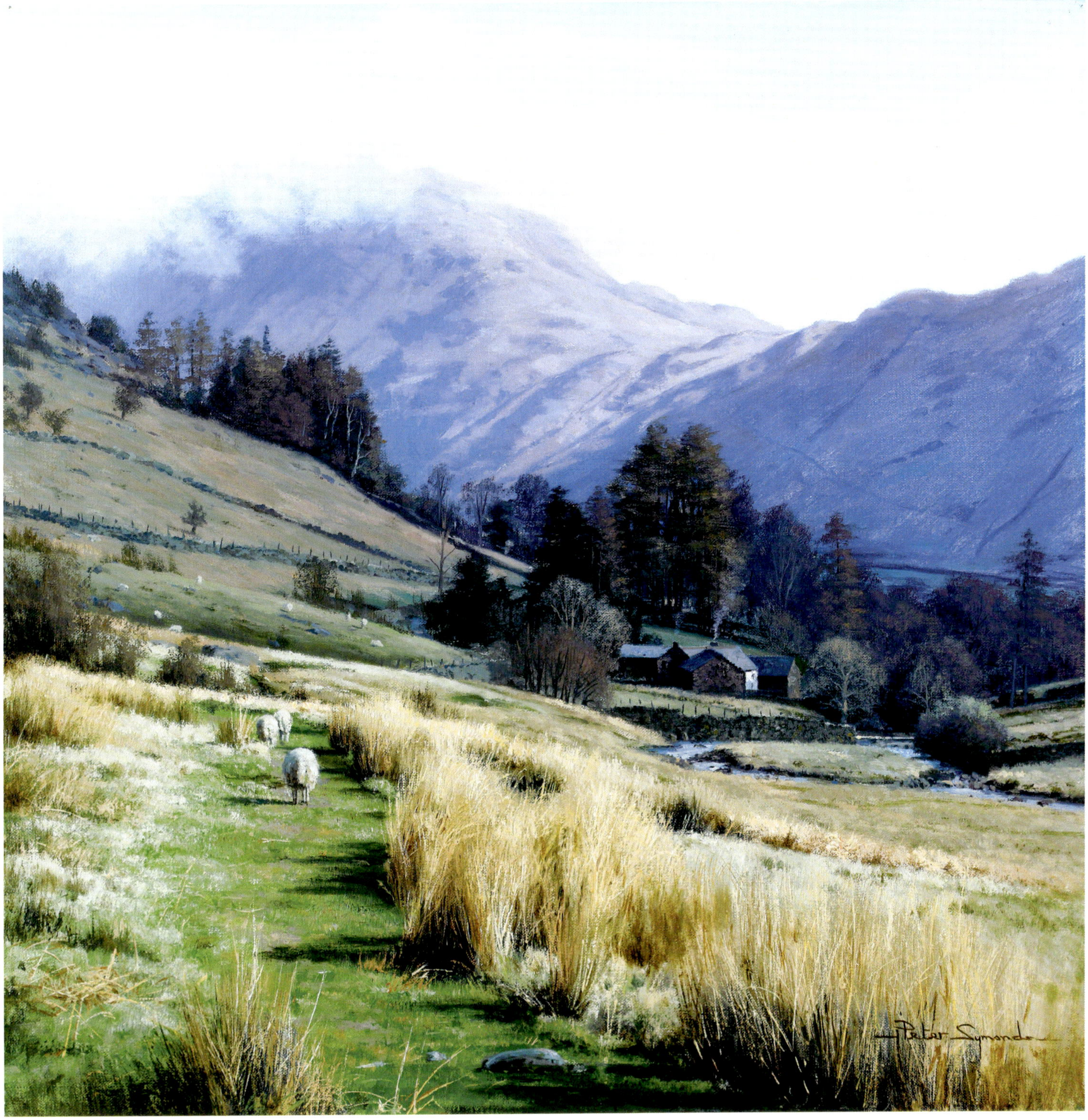
Peter Symonds

Stickle Ghyll and the Langdale Pikes

There are many scenes that I keep on the 'waiting to do' list, sometimes for many years until the conditions are just right to paint them. This view looks at its best in the afternoon and early evening when the shadows fall across the landscape. There is also the happy coincidence of the orange leaves on the tree standing out in front of the blue shadows on Harrison Stickle. Complementary colours always look more striking when placed near one another.

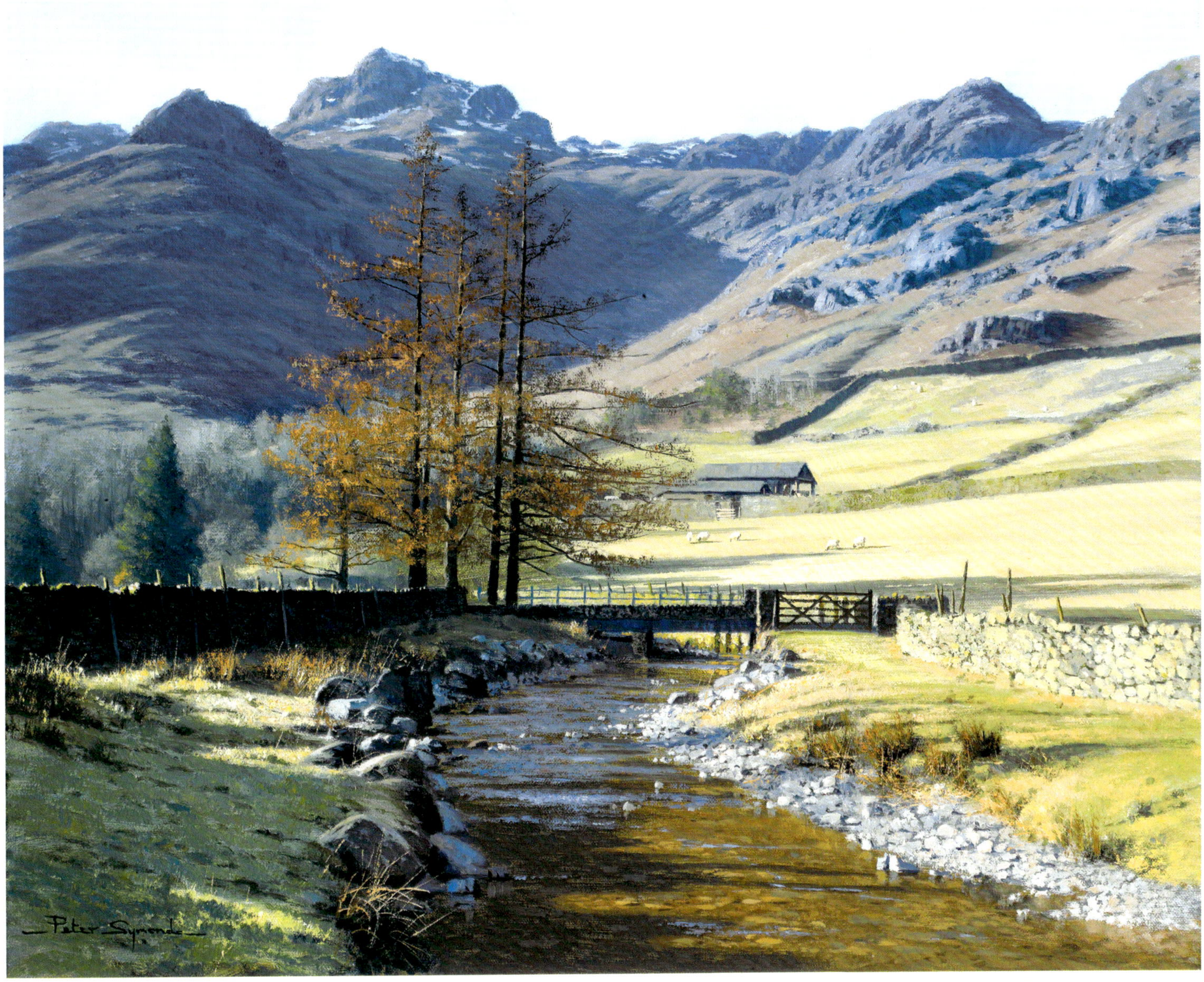
Peter Symonds

Spring in Grisedale

Over the years, we have rented a very picturesque old farmhouse about two miles up a track in Grisedale near Ullswater. The farm stands in wonderful isolation with superb views over to the ridge that eventually takes the walker up Striding Edge and onto Helvellyn. A few hundred metres beyond the house stands this lovely old barn. Despite knowing this view well, it was many years until the weather and light made it just right to paint.

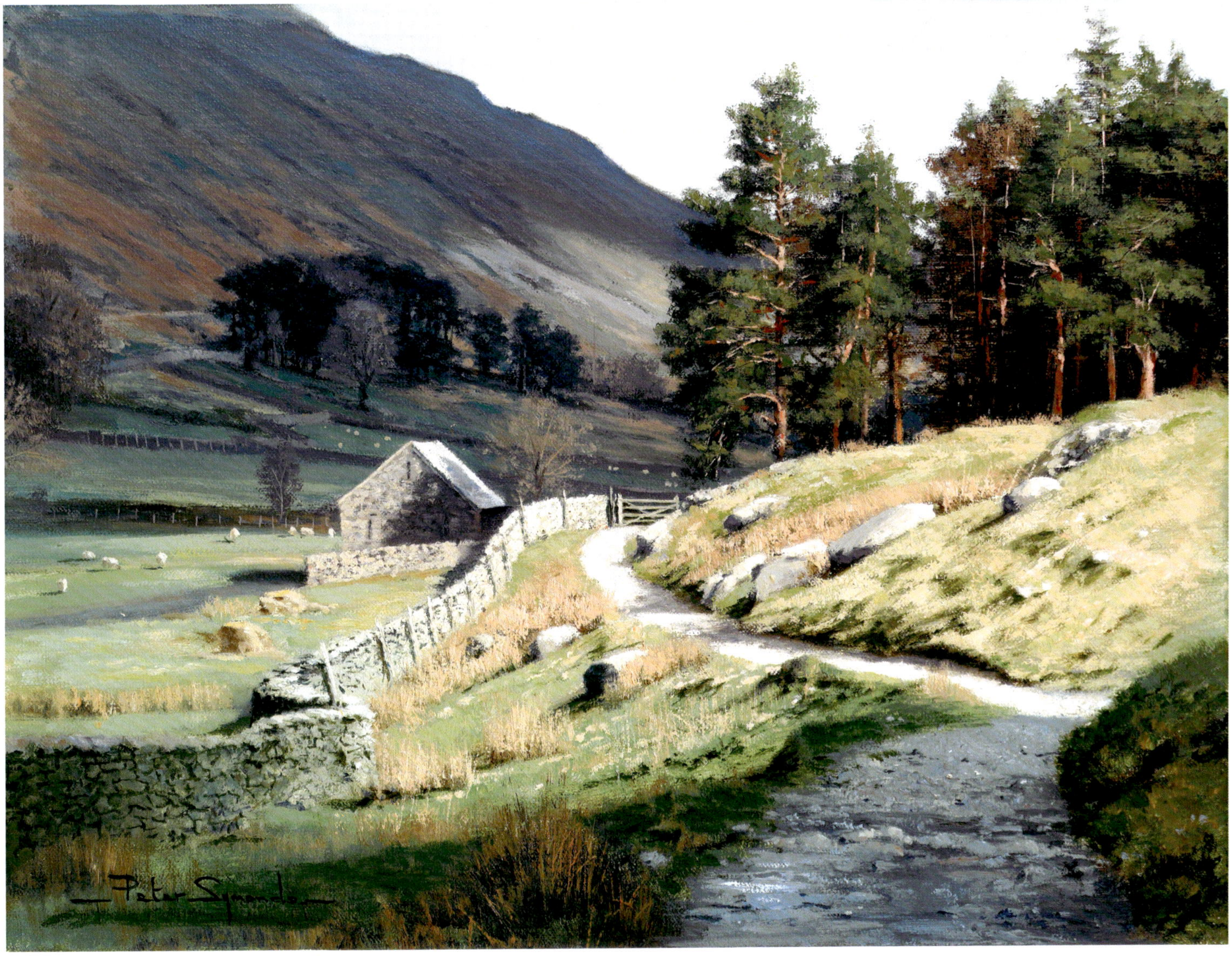

Low Hall Garth, Little Langdale

I have been told that this farmhouse was, until recently, inhabited by a farmer who only once left his native valley to visit the 'outside world' (and that was only to Ambleside!). I'm not sure if this is true, but if one had to be confined to a small valley I can think of few better places than this. Compared to neighbouring Great Langdale, this valley is a more peaceful place. Although the road through it can get busy – often with motorists on their way to and from the passes at Wrynose and Hardknott – the lack of places to stop and park the car means that few people get out to explore this lovely part of the Lakes.

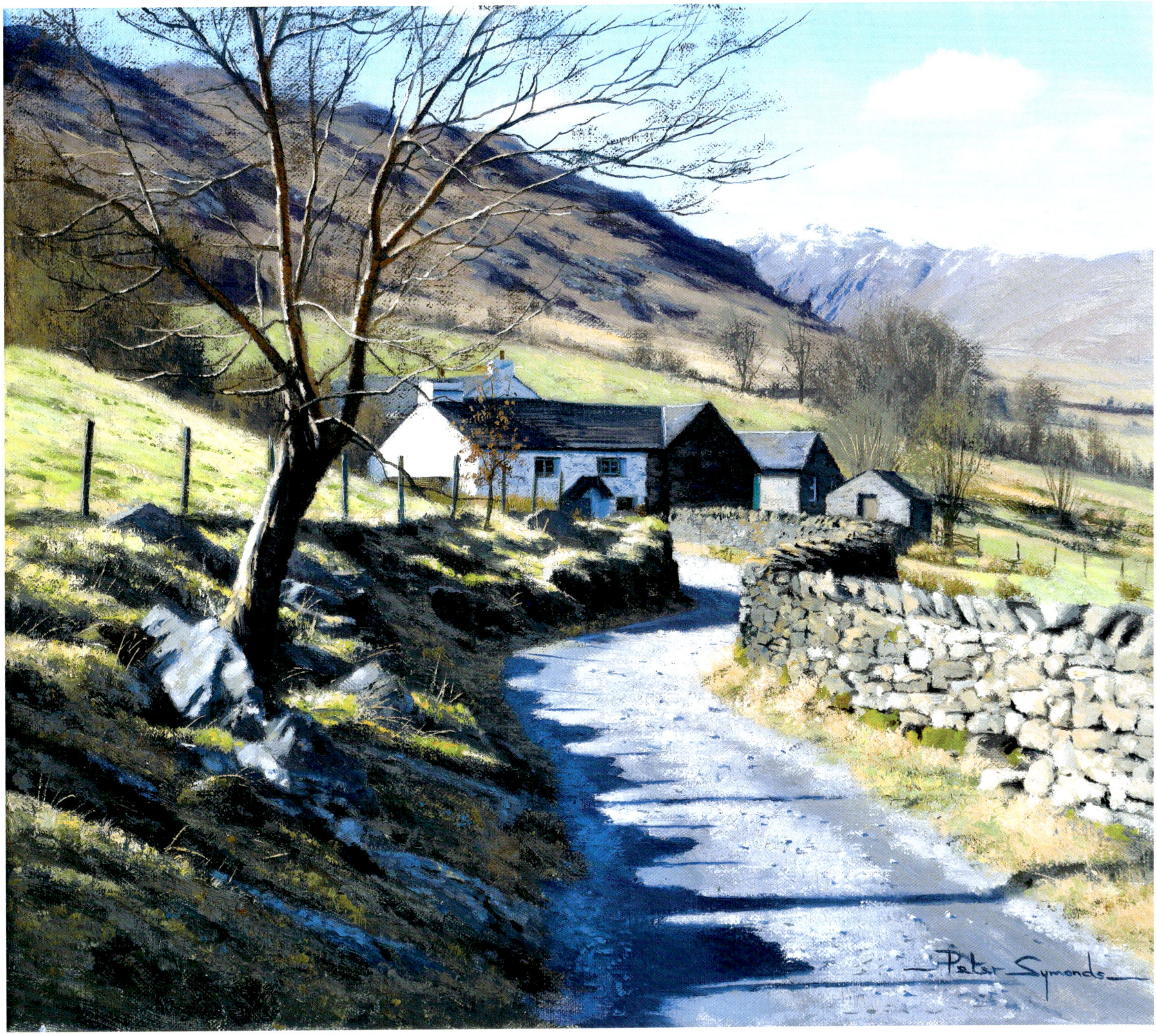
Peter Symonds

Black Moss Pot, Langstrath Valley

Many people who have had the joy of walking up the Langstrath Valley at the head of Borrowdale miss this little cleft in the rocks because it cannot be seen from the adjacent path. This is a pity, because it is a fine pool to swim in. A friend and I recently returned to the Langstrath after a long walk over from Eskdale to the south. It was early in May and we had enjoyed a fabulous sunny week camping out in the fells, but were weary as we approached the end of our trip. Ron's enthusiasm for leaping into any stretch of water was still unfettered, and I was impressed by his high dives into the deep pools below. Too cowardly to follow these exploits, I nevertheless relished another great swim and was soon revitalised for the last couple of miles walking back to the car.

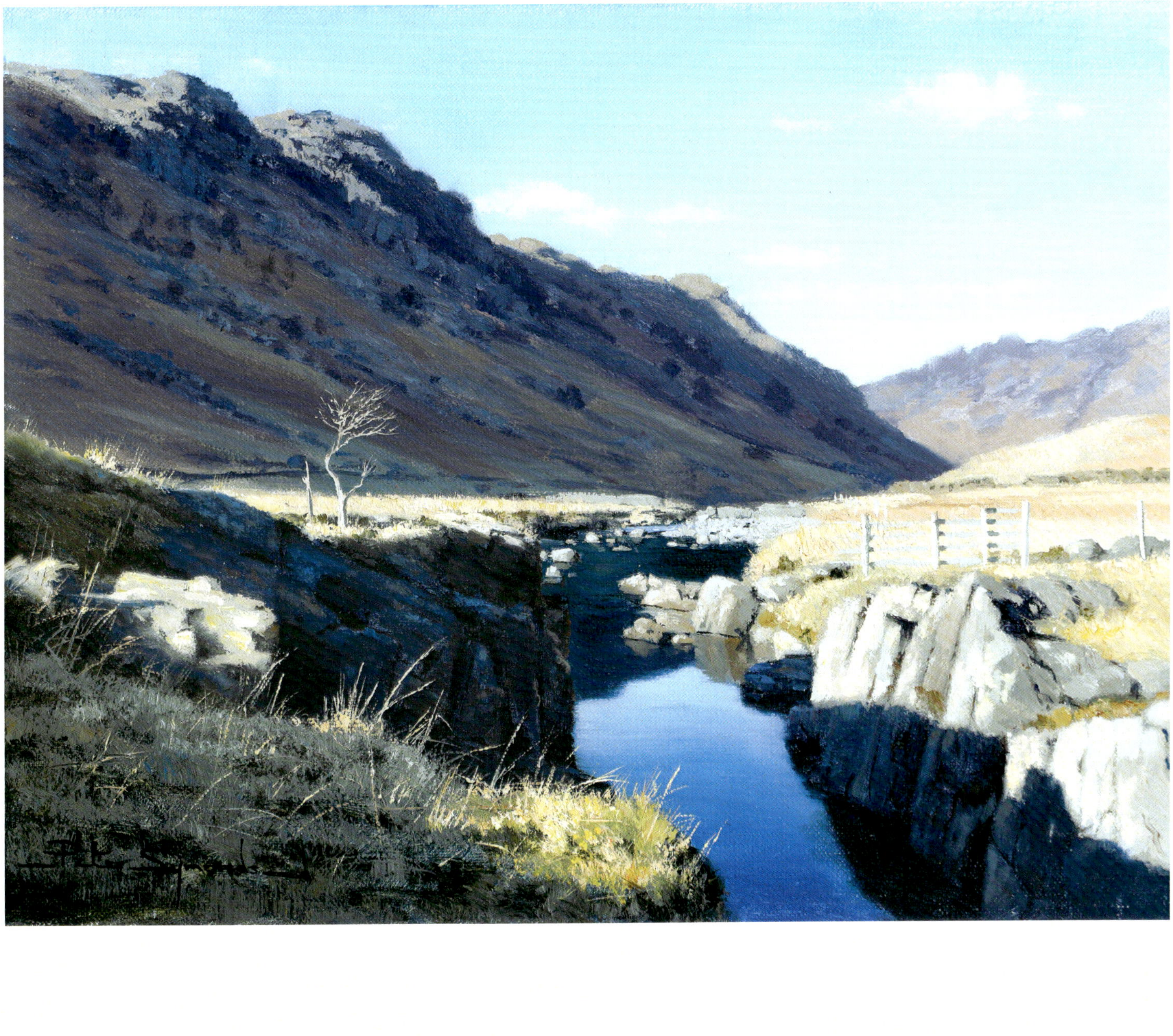

Clear Morning, Grisedale

The cold winter of 2009/2010 left the fells blanketed in snow until well into spring. There was a wonderful spell of clear, sunny weather in March and the whole area looked stunning. I have always loved this view looking up at the valley, and with Dollywagon Pike under snow it looked particularly good.

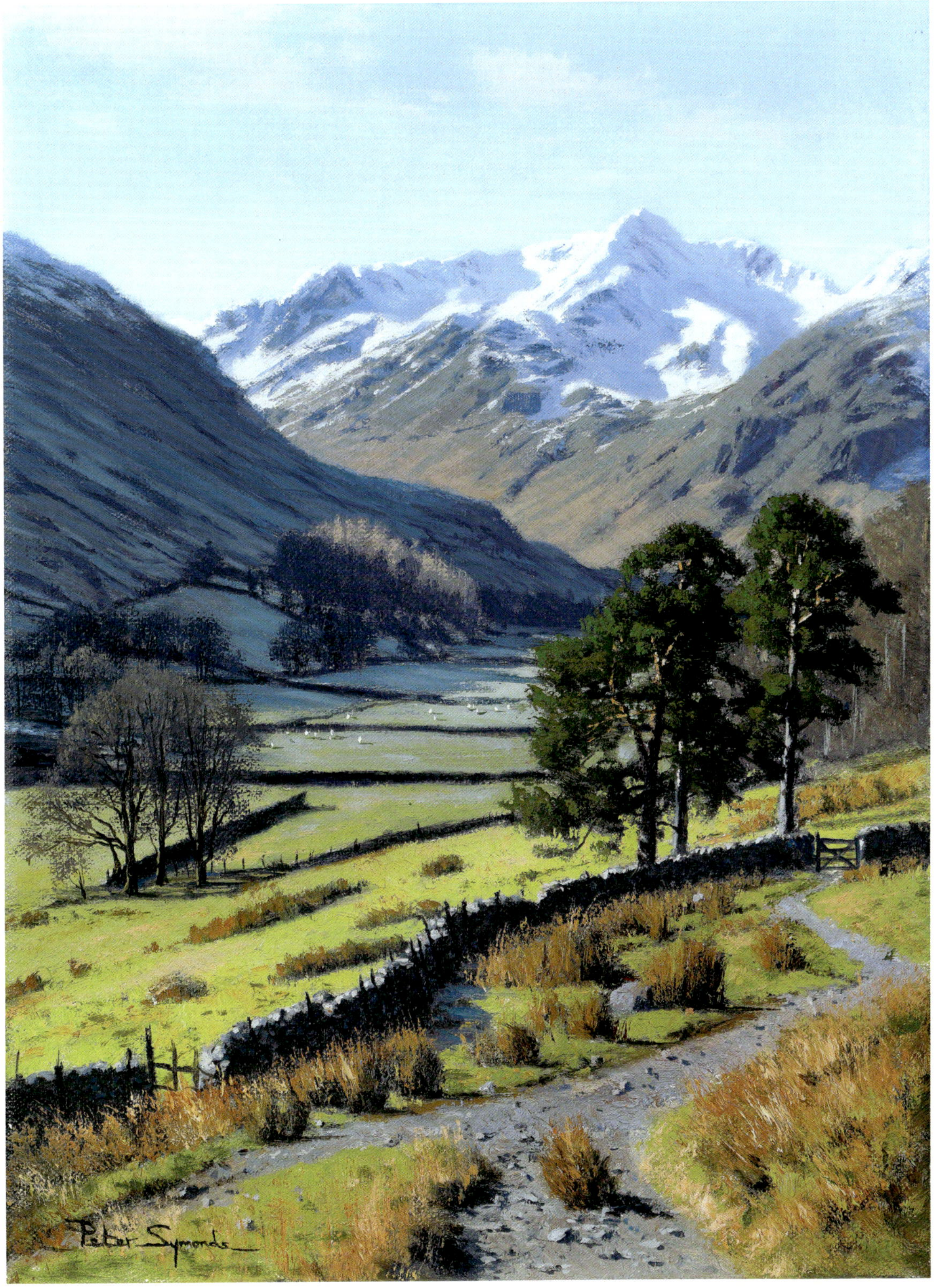
Peter Symonds

A Frosty Morning, Grange-in-Borrowdale

The bridges and river at Grange-in-Borrowdale have to be one of the most painted and photographed locations in Lakeland. One of the reasons for this is that they stand right beside the road that heads up to Borrowdale. This was a bitterly cold morning and not a time to linger any longer than necessary.

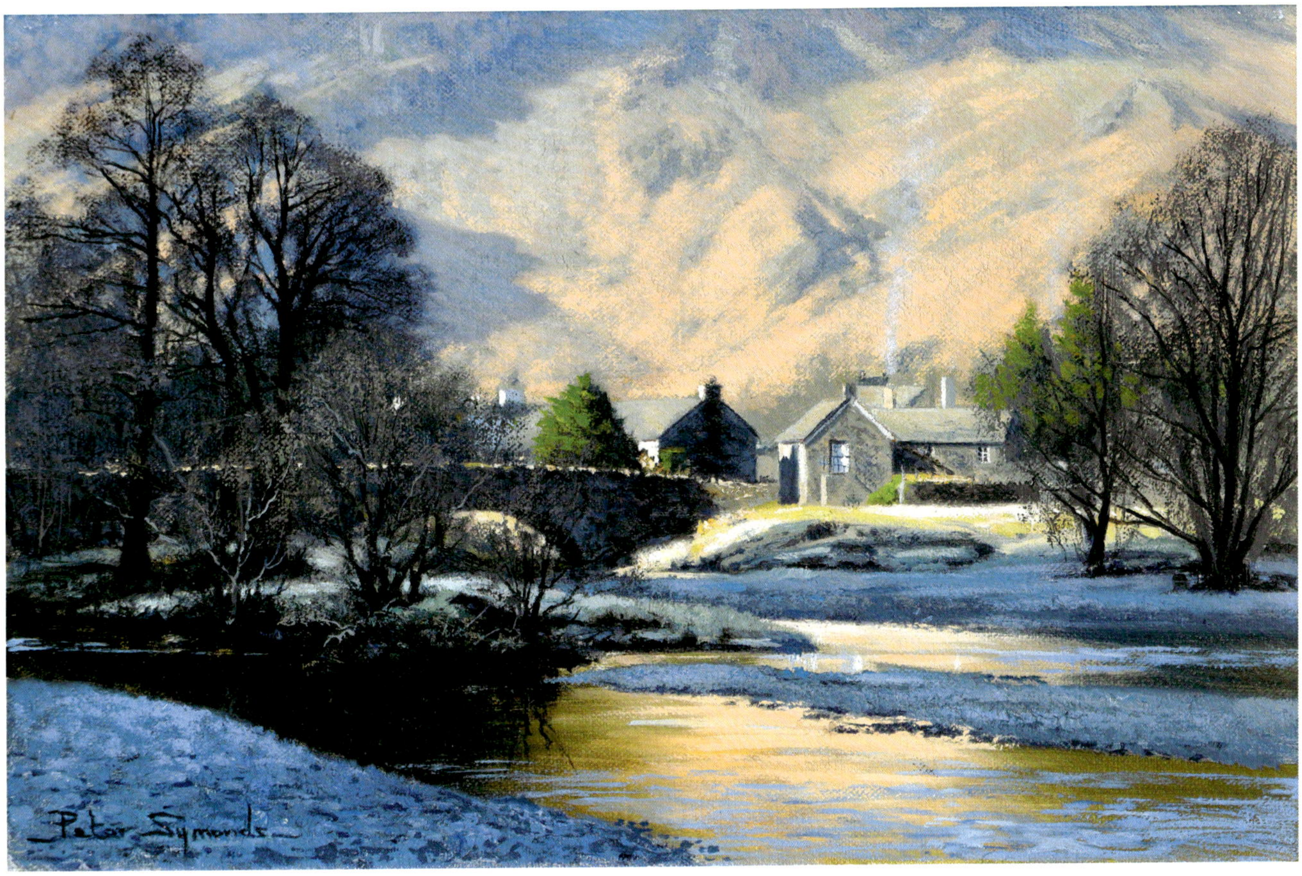
Peter Symonds

The Gables from Innominate Tarn

I have never quite understood why this lovely tarn should be given this 'nameless' title when it does in fact have an old original name – Loaf Tarn. Not a great name, agreed, but surely better than its current one. This tarn and the neighbouring fell of Haystacks were so beloved by the late Alfred Wainwright that he chose to have his ashes scattered by its shore.

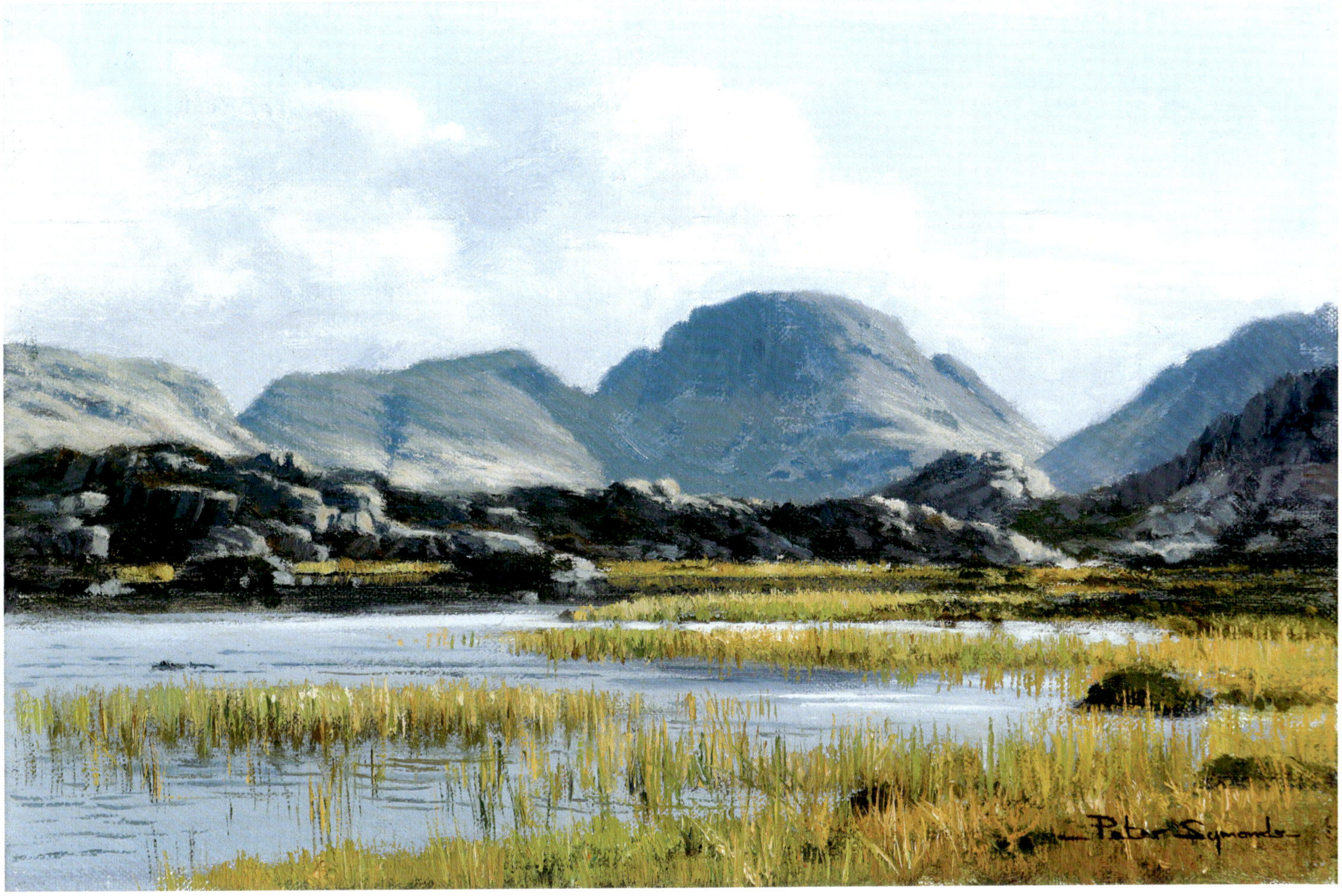
Peter Symonds

Skiddaw from Newlands Beck

A walk up the lovely Newlands Valley with a return via Hindscarth, Robinson or High Spy makes a great outing. The beck constantly transforms itself as it tumbles down from Dalehead Tarn and there is a delightful waterfall about a mile from the col.

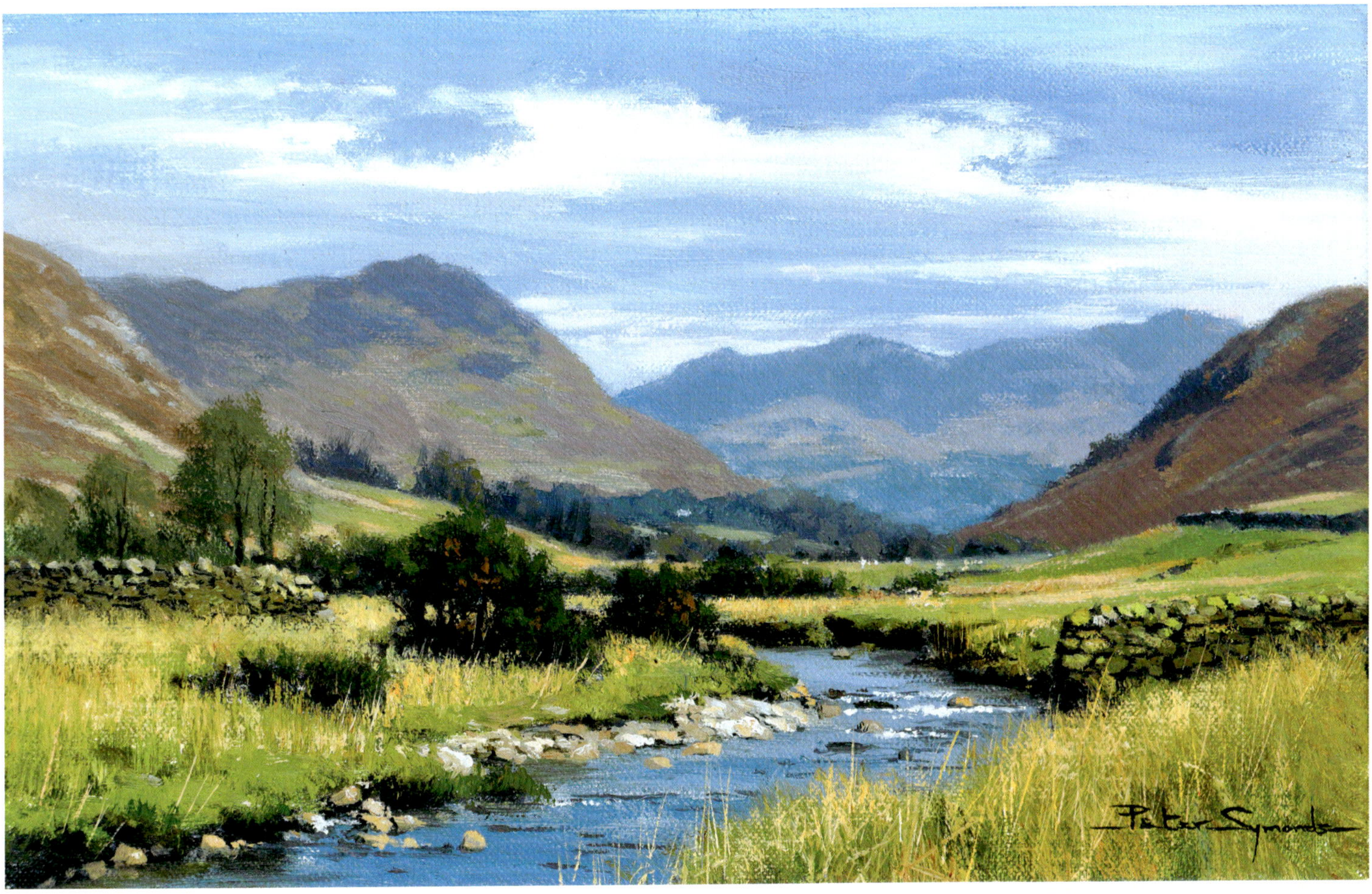
Peter Symonds

Crinkle Crags and Bowfell from Red Tarn

The traverse of the wonderfully named Crinkle Crags and the climb up to Bowfell beyond makes a superb outing for the fell walker. Beneath the rocky summits of Pike O'Blisco and Cold Pike, at about 1700ft, nestles this beautiful shallow tarn. It looks at its best in the autumn months when the reeds and golden grasses along the shore light up the foreground and compliment the craggy fell beyond.

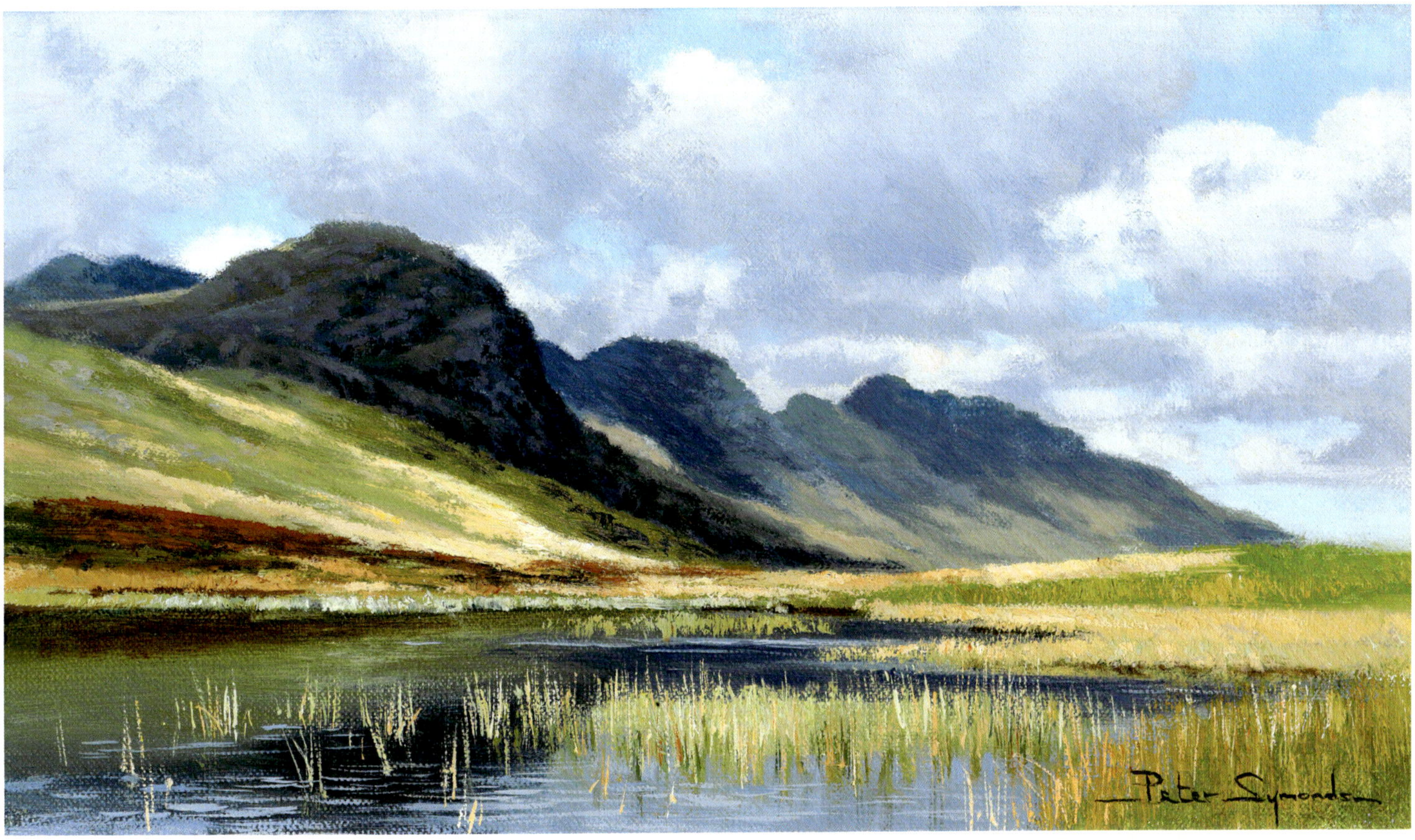
Peter Symonds

River Brathay near Ambleside

With so many of the becks in the Lake District tumbling off the fells amongst jagged rocks and boulders, it is almost a surprise to find a river like this languidly flowing past banks of reeds and fields. This was a wonderful little subject to paint and was enhanced by the hazy light that gives the painting so much more depth.

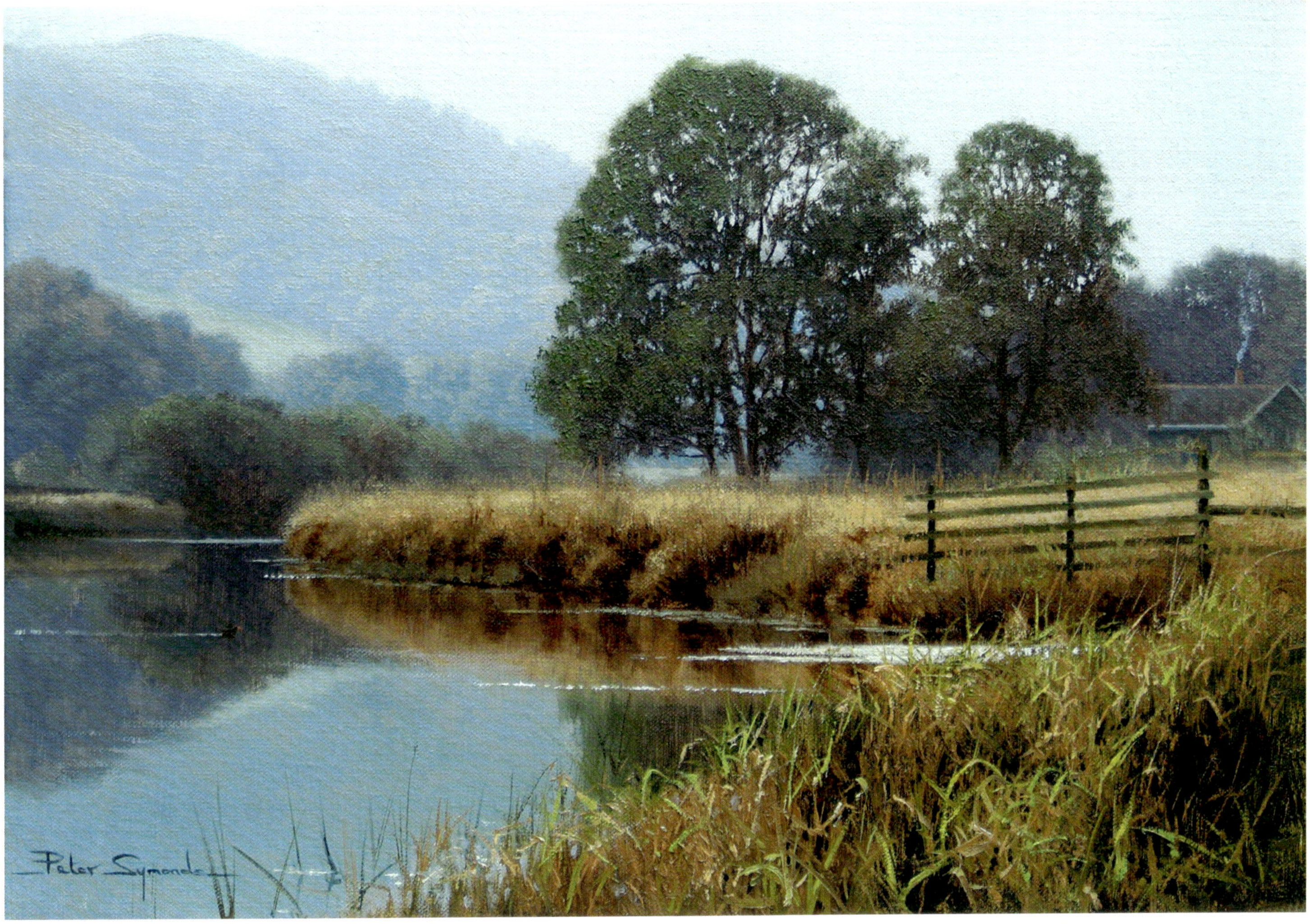
Peter Symonds

River Brathay near Elterwater

The walk between Elterwater and Skelwith Bridge is a deservedly popular route, as for nearly two miles one is able to closely follow the banks of the river Brathay and Elterwater, a lovely low-lying tarn with great views up to the Langdale Pikes in the distance. I have chosen a view looking south-west across the river towards the low fells at the foot of Little Langdale.

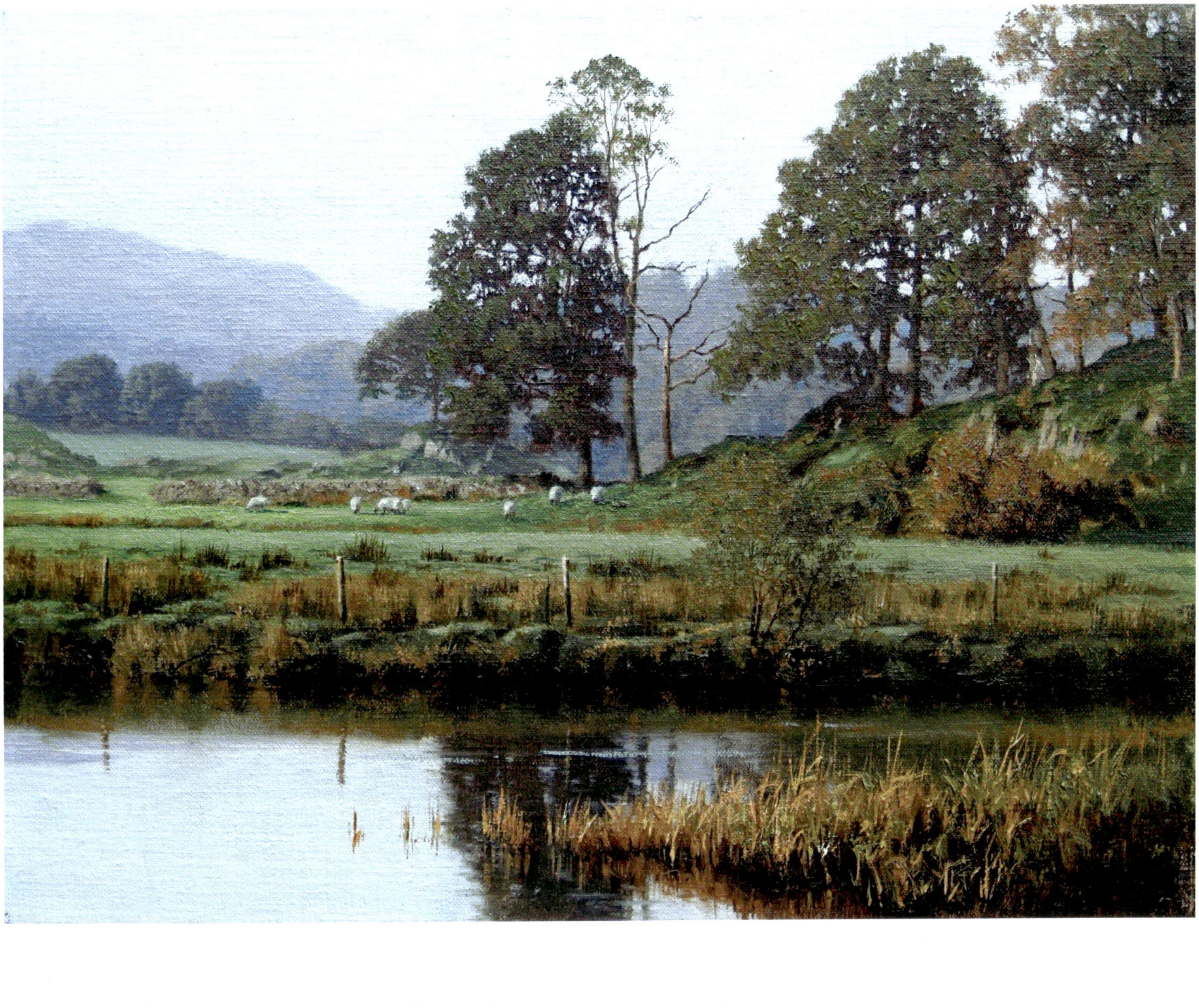

Bright Beck and Stickle Tarn

Stickle Tarn makes an interesting and dramatic picture from most angles, but I love this view from the little beck that flows into it from the north. An invaluable aid to creating an interesting composition is using a track or stream, as here, to allow the viewer's eye to travel through the painting from the foreground to the distant horizon.

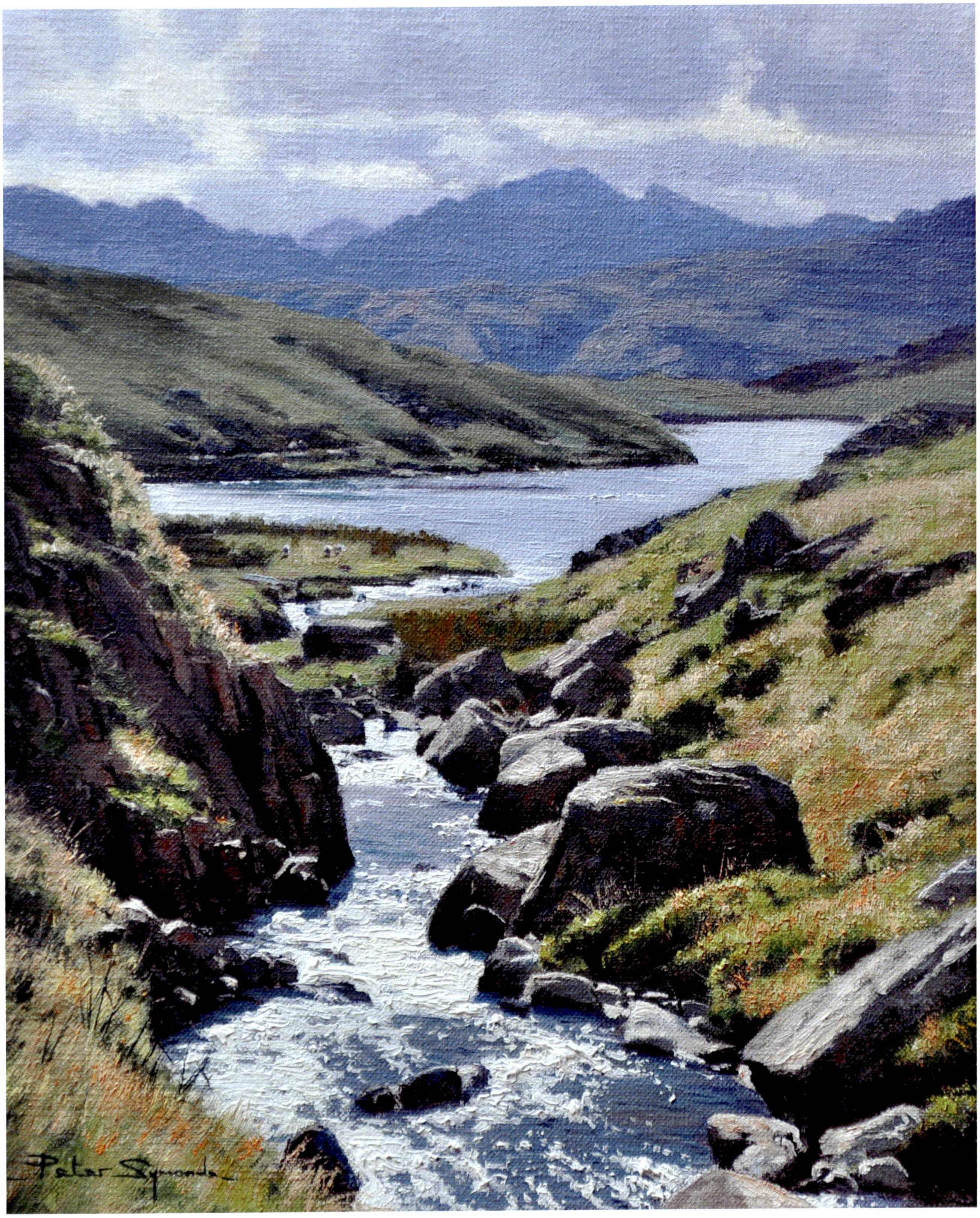
Peter Symonds

Easedale Tarn

The walk up to Easedale Tarn from Grasmere is one of the busiest routes in the Lake District for those who prefer not to climb onto the fells or who are kept down by inclement weather. I have walked around the tarn and found it a difficult subject to paint until I climbed up the banks of Slapestone Edge, from where it makes a far more pleasing subject. Yet again, I was helped by the clouds scudding across the sky, allowing the sun to illuminate some of the fells while casting their neighbours into shadow – giving that all-important atmosphere one seeks to capture.

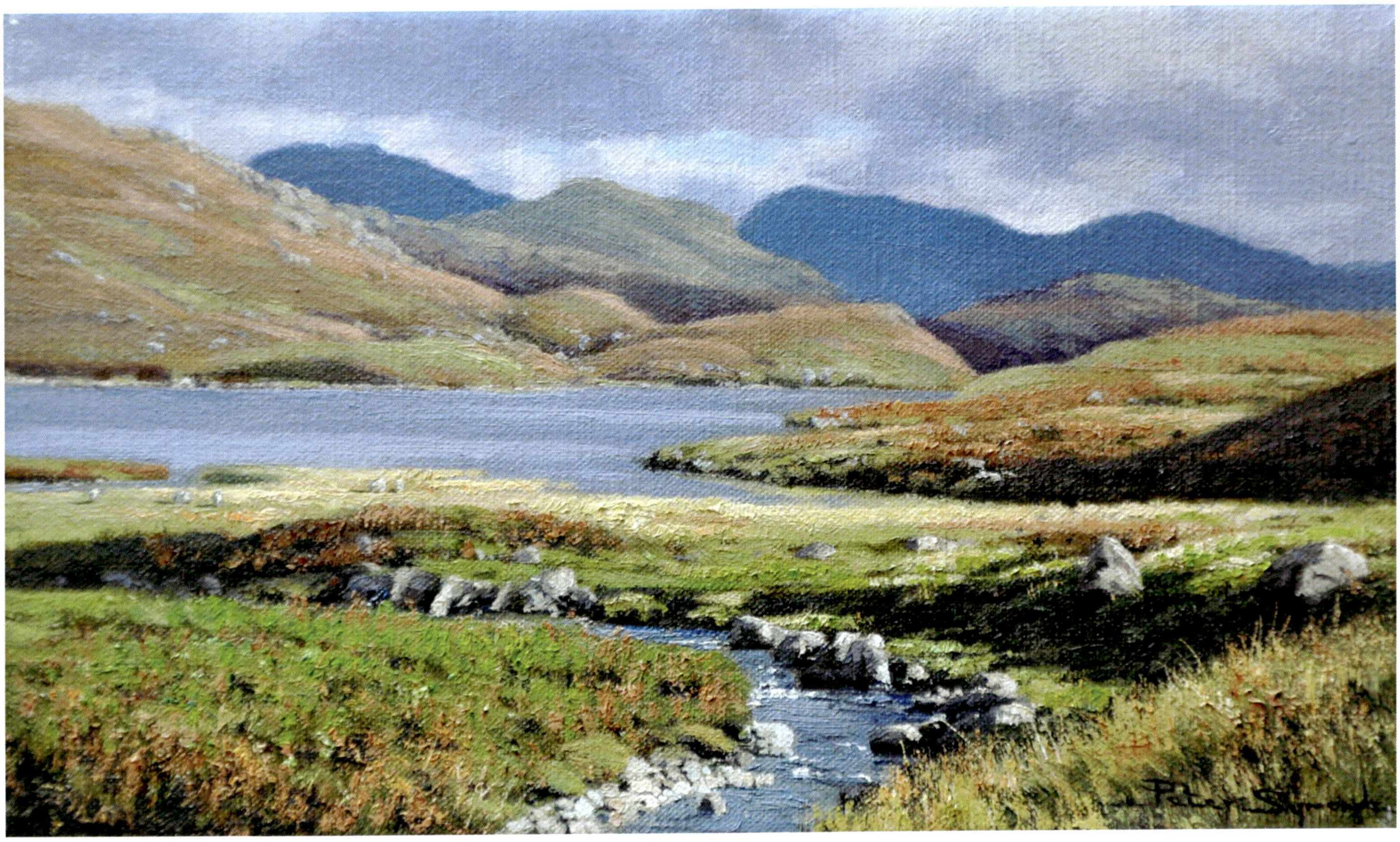

Old Oak beside Crummock Water

I have always loved to paint studies of solitary trees, and this is a magnificent example of a battered old oak beside the east shore of Crummock Water. It has obviously seen better days, as the branches littered at its feet testify, but I feel the more open shape gives it great character.

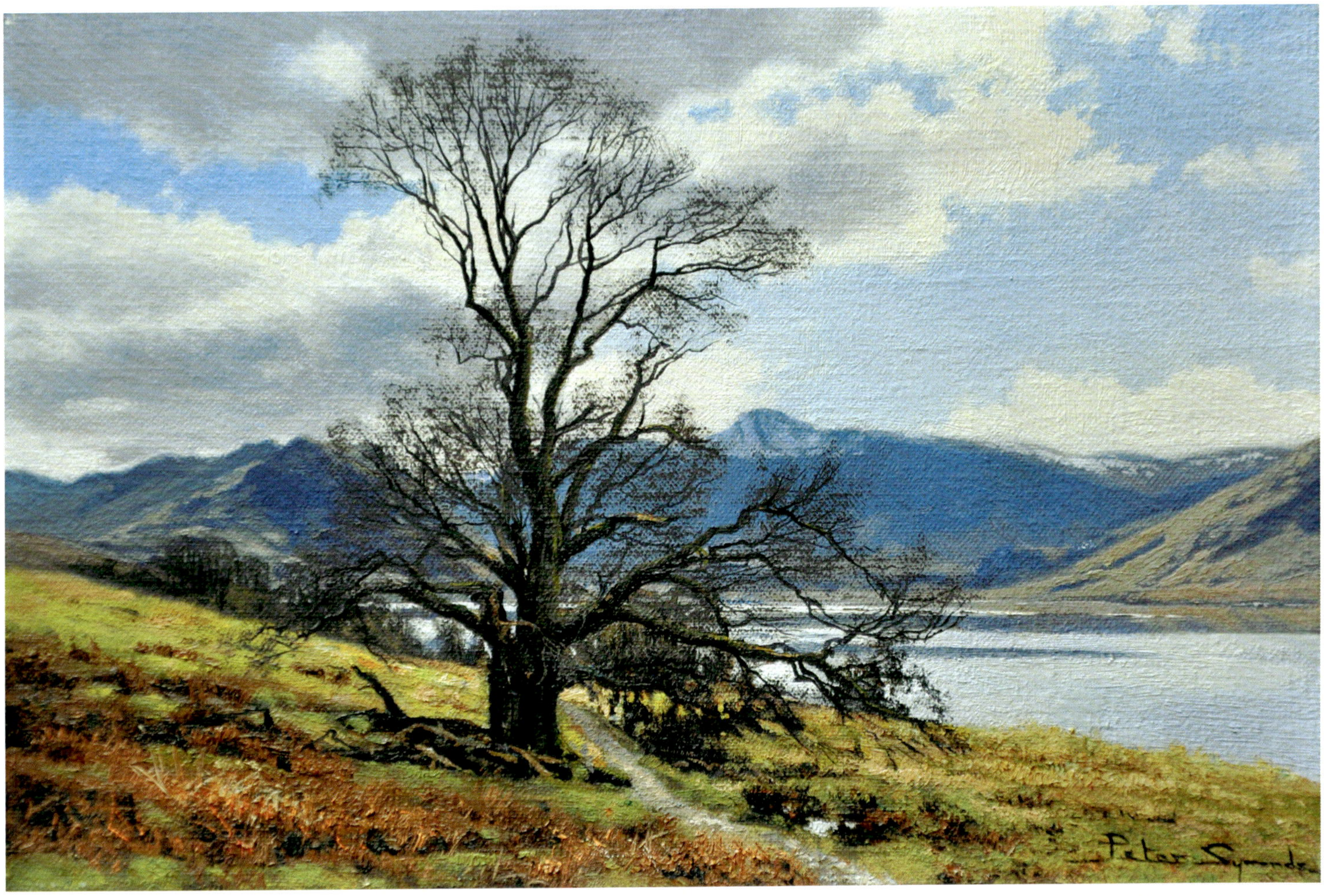
Peter Symonds

Elm How, Grisedale

Over the years my family and I have stayed in this beautiful old farmhouse, and we have many fond memories of our times here. There is a little waterfall in the woods, and off the picture to the right is a lovely old bridge which spans Grisedale Beck. It is a superb place for children to play as there are no cars that pass by. As I write this we are going back in a week's time – I can't wait!

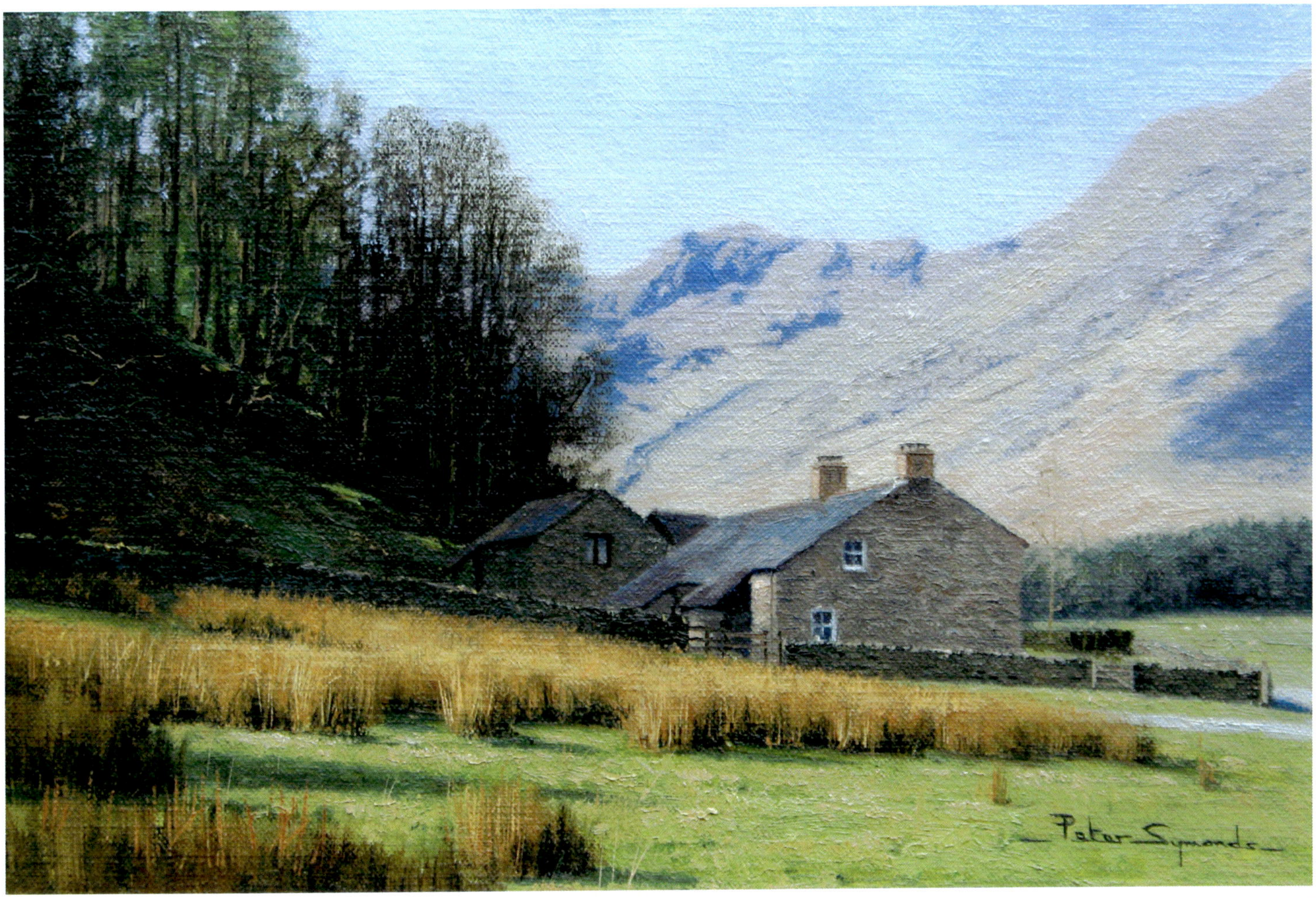
Peter Symonds

The Open Gate

A good composition is vital for making an interesting painting, and over the centuries painters and writers have attempted to formularise classic compositional structures. Generally, in seeking subjects to paint, I don't pay too much attention to these laws and go instinctively for scenes that just feel right and have a good balance about them. The painting here, however, is what teachers would call an L-shaped composition, with the strong vertical of the tree to the left and the horizontals of the barn and wall to the right. This does give the painting here a good balance, but what is just as important is the track up to and through the open gate, which allows the viewer's eye to move through the painting. The sheep, which were painted from memory, help give the composition a good focal point too.

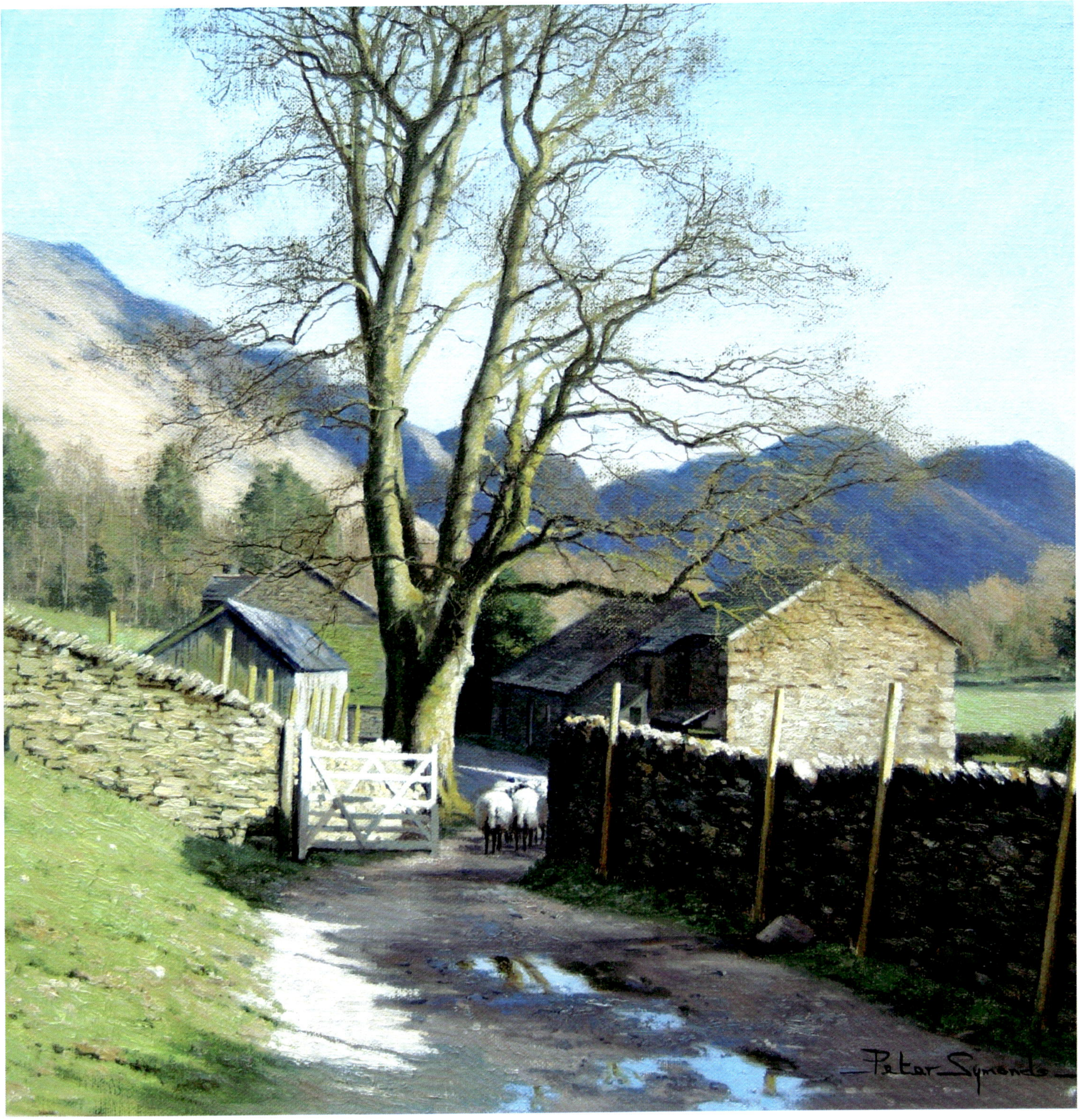
Peter Symonds

Whose Right of Way?

There was never really going to be a stand-off here, but this character was not as timid as so many of her kind.

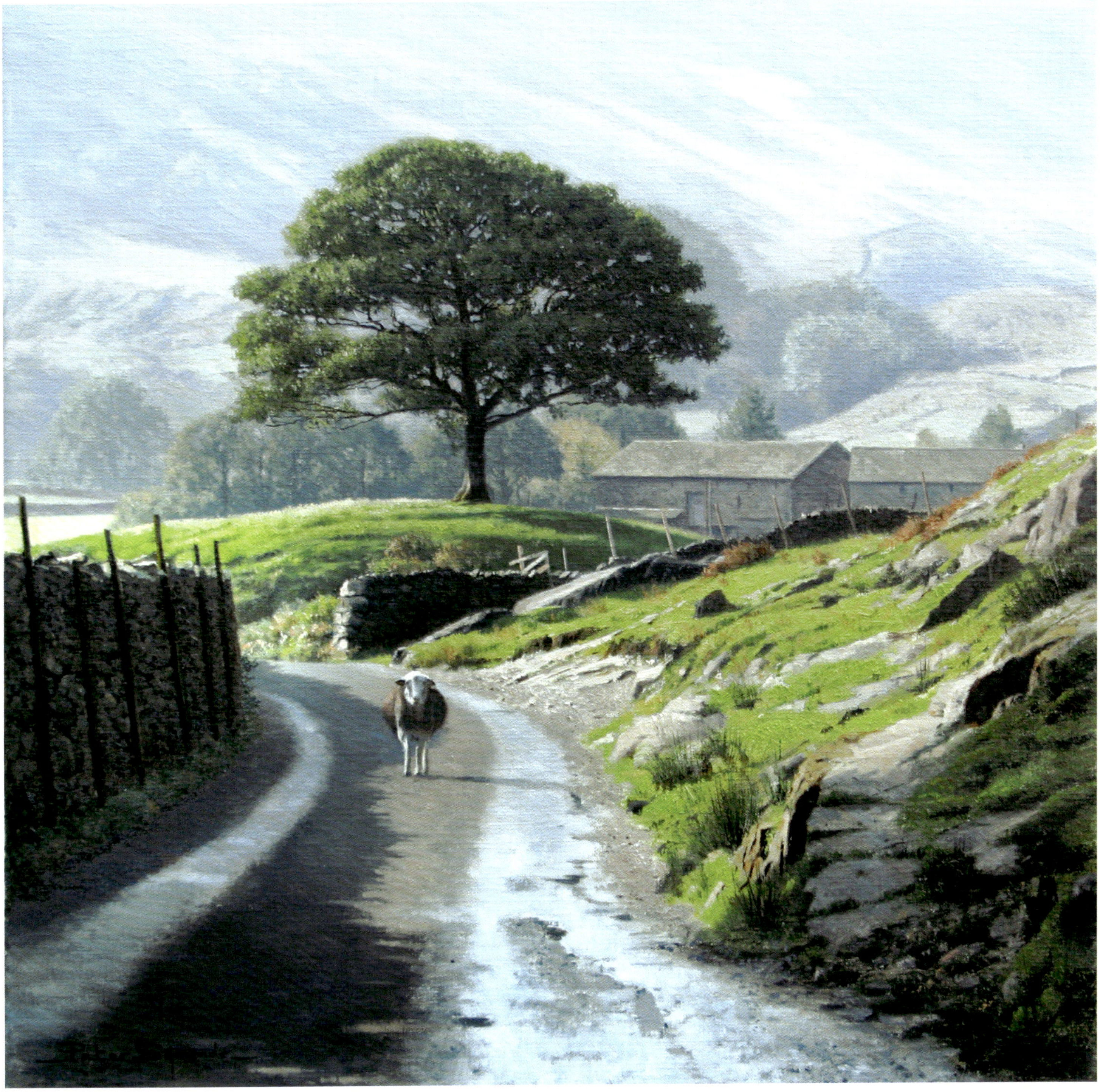

Jaws of Borrowdale

As it is fed by quite a few named tributaries to the south, I have never been quite sure where the river Derwent first takes on its own identity, but it is probably at Seatoller. Initially it flows through the wide, flat valley of Borrowdale, but a mile or so south of Grange the valley narrows significantly as the fells to the west and east crowd in on the river. This beautiful spot, where there is a great walk through mixed woodland, is the wonderfully named 'Jaws of Borrowdale'. There is an amusing anecdote on the sale of the painting as it was sold to a couple I know, one of whom is a dentist!

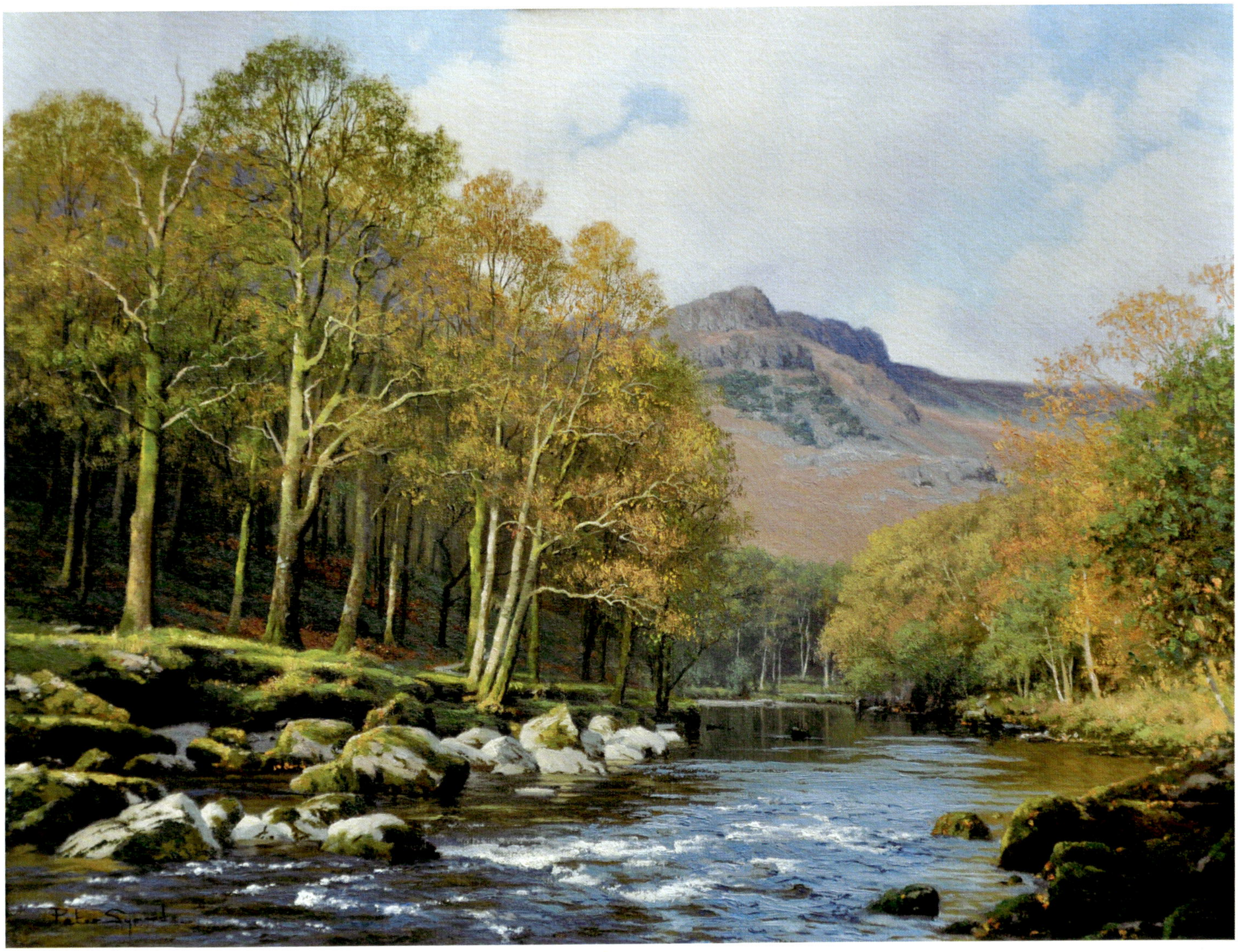

Millbeck and the Langdale Pikes

This scene epitomises why I so love to paint the Lake District. Everything is just so naturally in the right place and very little artistic licence is needed. However, if the farmhouse was not there, providing a superb focal point, the whole painting would have failed. Generally the focal point should never be dead centre on the canvas, but artists never have to be slaves to rules if that helps our cause.

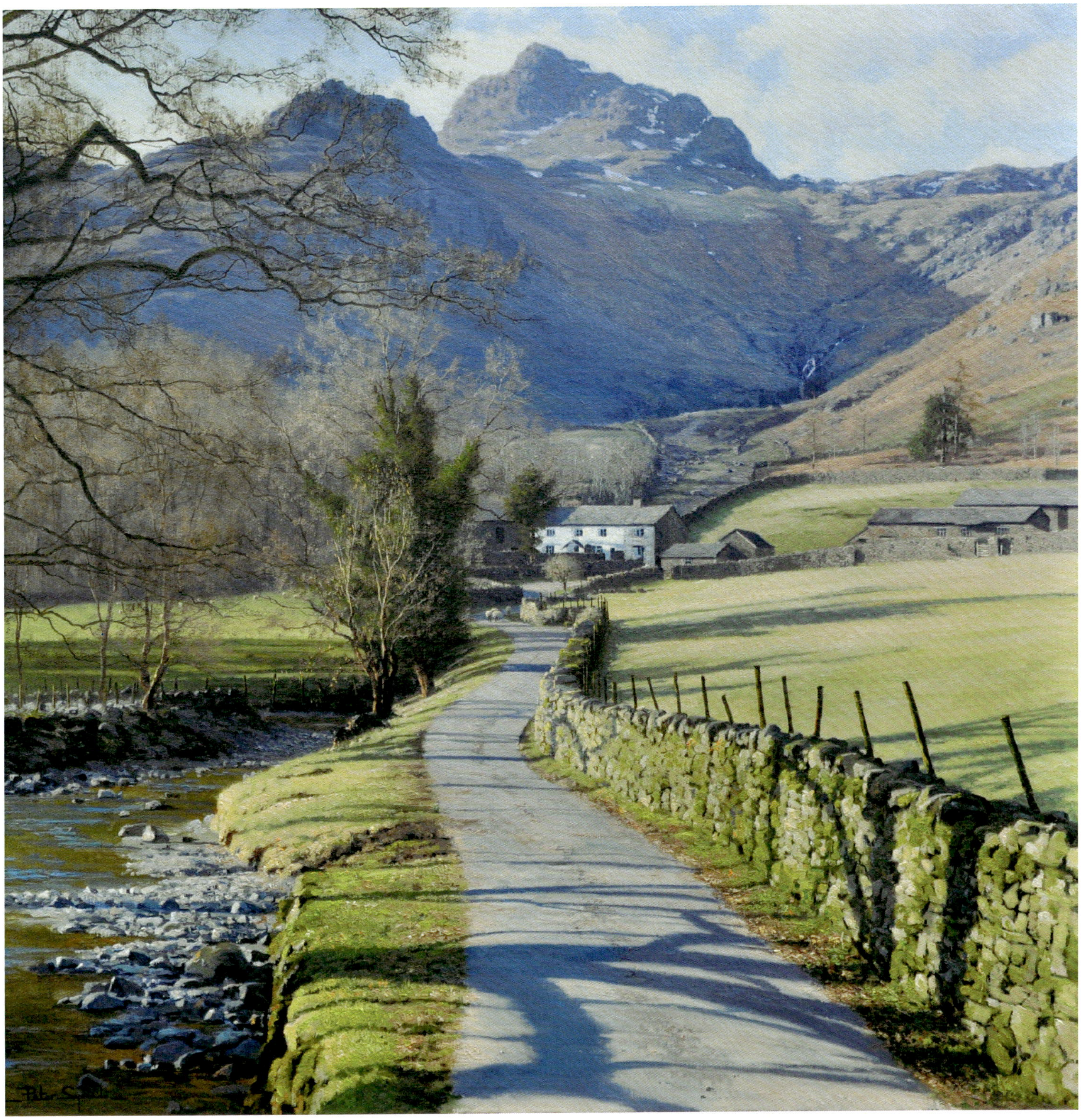

Patterdale

I think it is important and helpful for a landscape artist to paint a wide range of scenery, as it is otherwise all too easy to stagnate or become bored if new challenges are not taken on to draw you out of your comfort zone. I do enjoy painting street scenes when I am abroad, but usually there is not too much evidence of man's presence in my paintings of the Lakes, except the occasional farmhouse or dry stone wall. This painting of Patterdale is about as 'urbanised' as I get when in the Lake District, but I hope the natural scenery still takes priority.

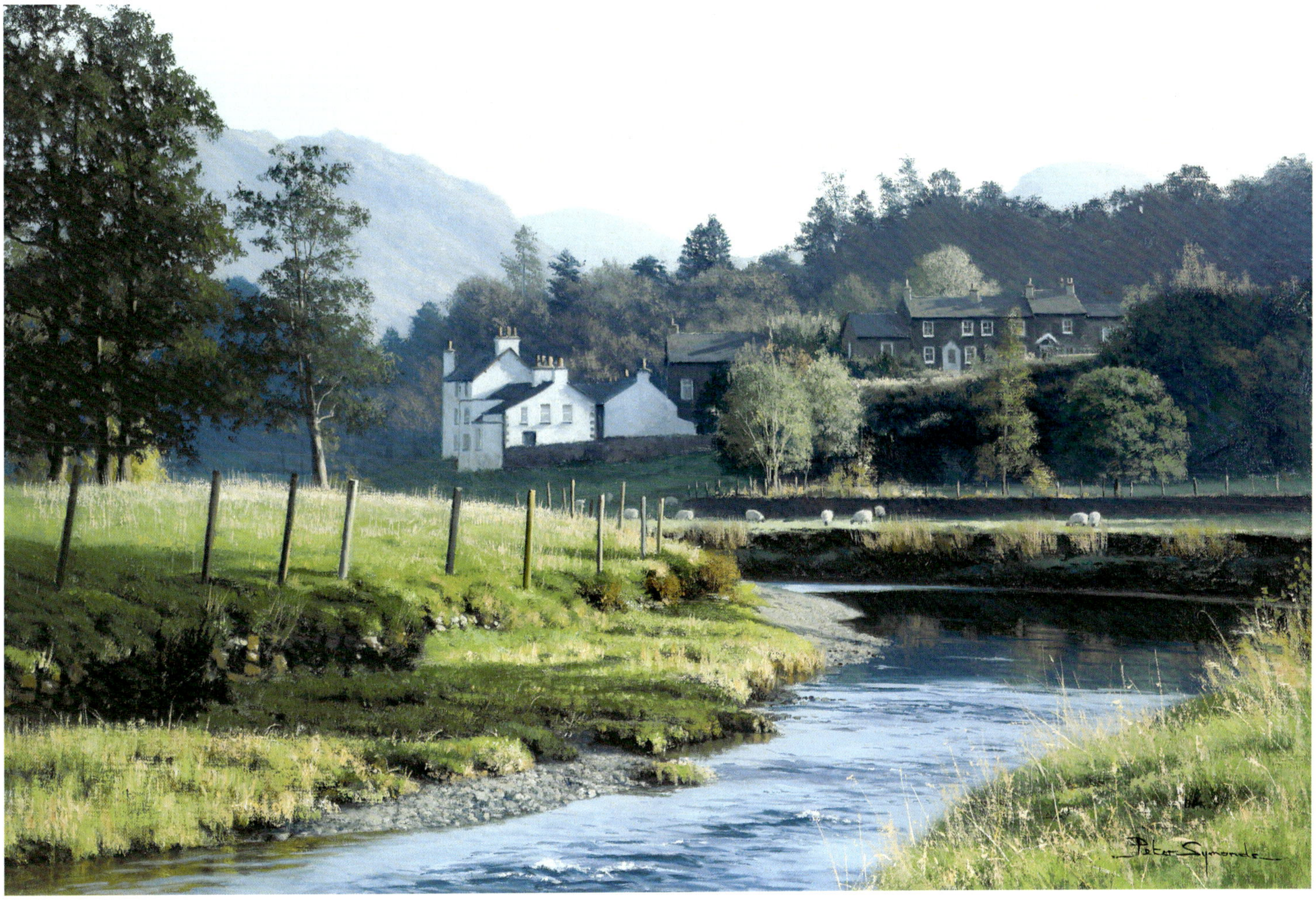

The Path to Eagle Crag, near Stonethwaite

I always think of this particular spot as the gateway to the beautiful Langstrath Valley that lies beyond. Before rushing onwards, this is also a delightful place to stop and linger, as just to the left of the painting there is a beautiful pool with accompanying waterfall – Galleny Force. It also gives a great view of Eagle Crag, one of the few fells in the area I have yet to explore.

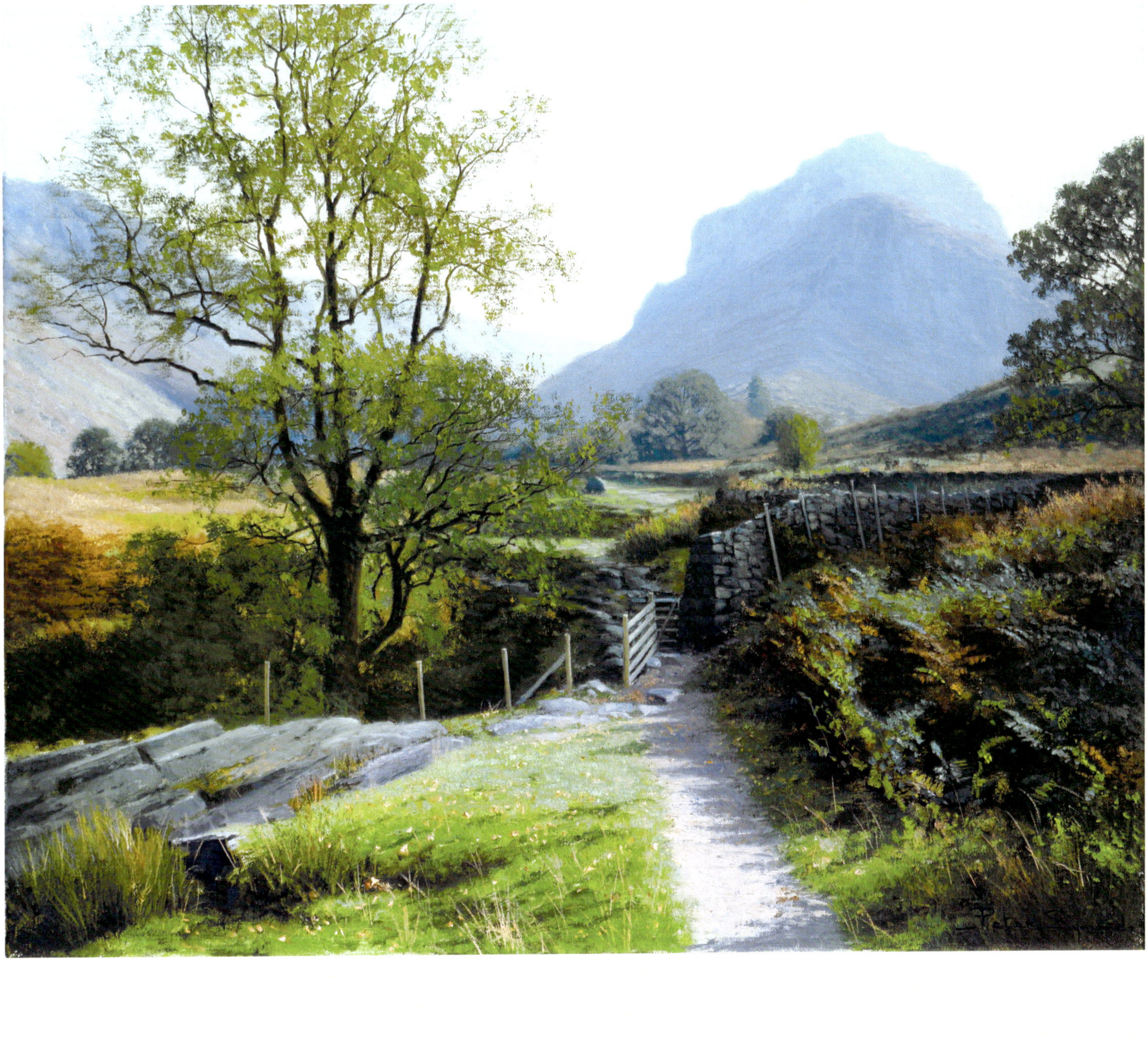

Swan Dub, Langstrath

This is another of the beautiful pools along the Langstrath that are so good to swim in. On several occasions in late April and early May, I have been surprised to find just how quickly the water warms up given a few days of sun, even though there can still be a bit of snow on the peaks.

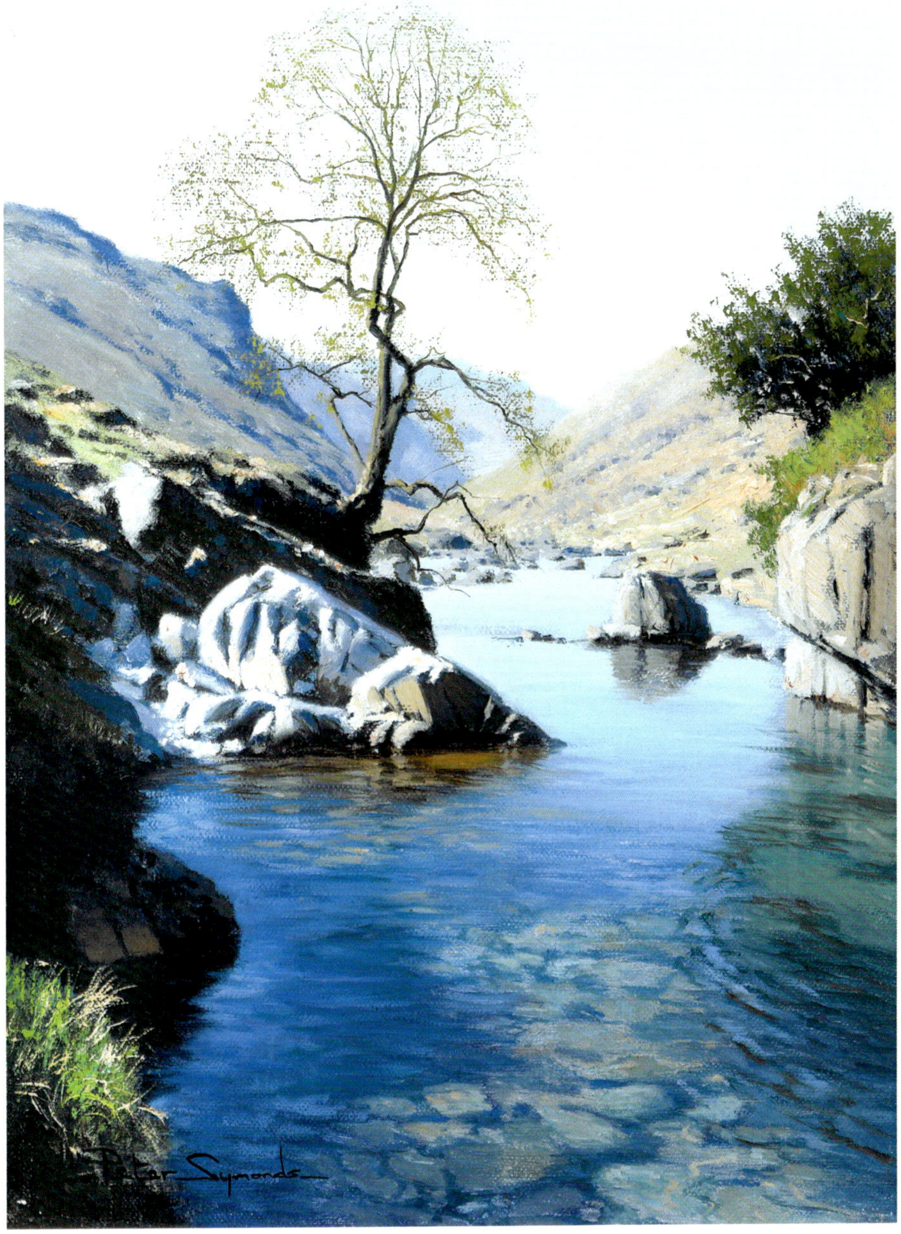

Langdale Pikes from Bridgend, Little Langdale

This is another of the classic whitewashed farms that are now owned by the National Trust, who do such a good job of preserving and looking after this beautiful corner of our country. Whoever first decided to settle at this particular location chose well – even if it was not for aesthetic reasons. The lovely Greenburn Beck flows just behind the buildings and the views in a 360 degree arc are simply breathtaking.

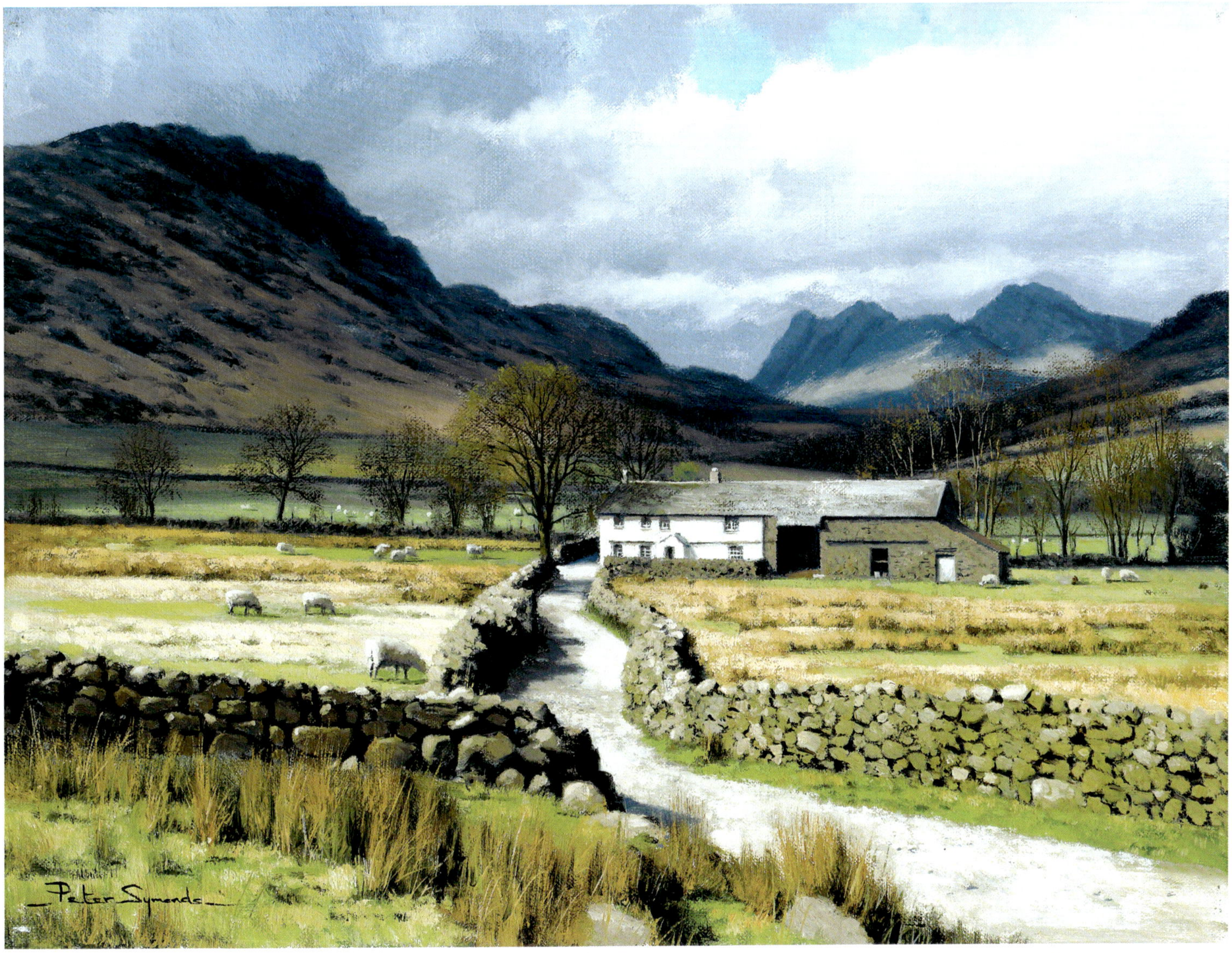
Peter Symonds

The Langdale Pikes, Late Summer

This was painted in early October, before the autumnal colours had reached the trees in the valley. This was one of the largest paintings I have undertaken and it was great fun trying to create the rough textures of the wall in heavy impasto paint. I have only ever painted in oils and feel it is the ideal medium with which to express oneself. They are also far more forgiving to use than watercolours. I feel you need a very systematic and organised approach when painting with watercolour, as if you get your tones or colours wrong with the first washes there is very little room to correct the painting without turning the colours muddy. With oil paint, if one gets a passage wrong it can be scraped off and then, by leaving it to dry, can be painted over. I also love the buttery consistency of oil paint, and the endless ways it can be manipulated with the brush onto the canvas.

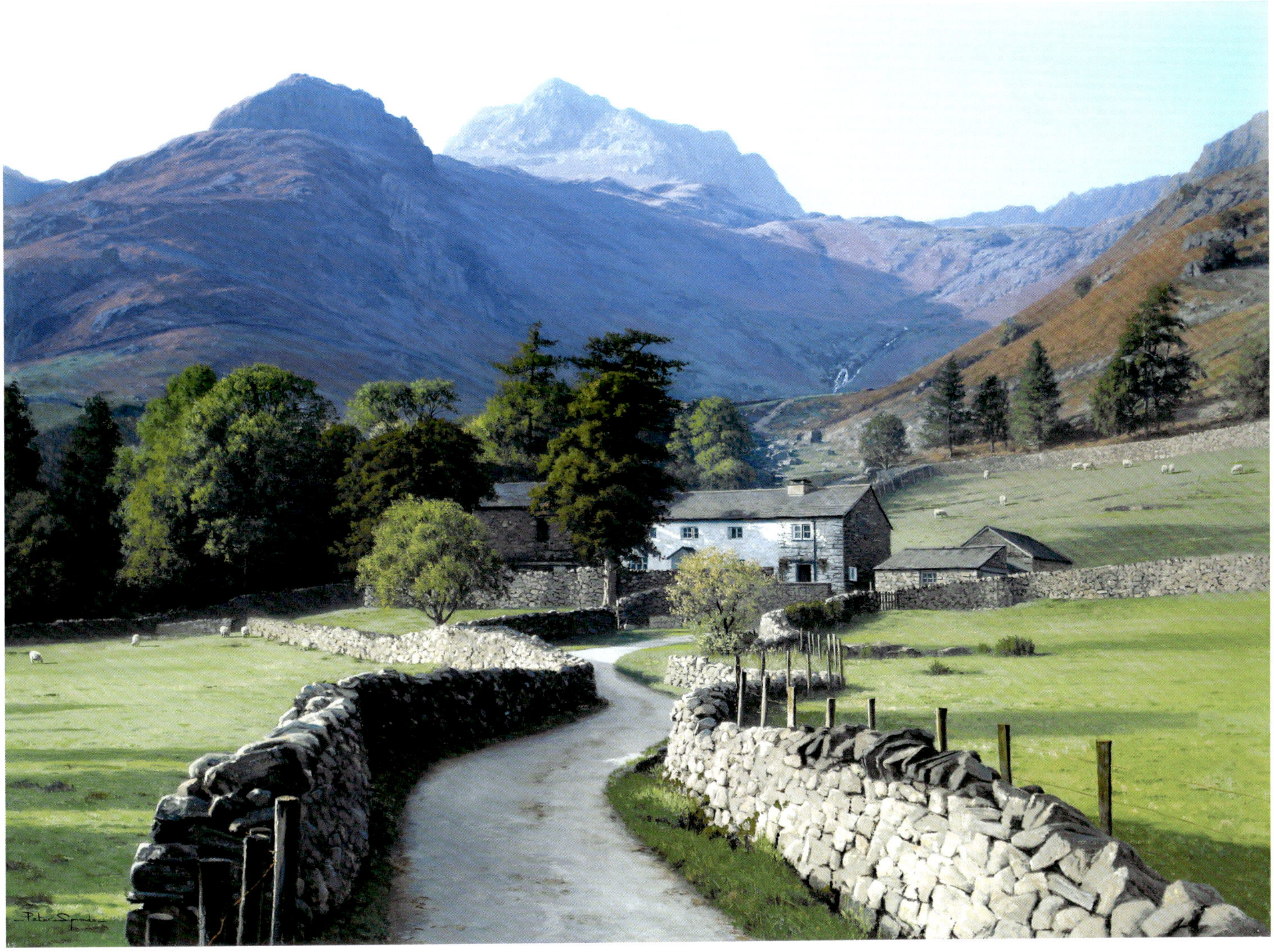

The Path to Howtown, Ullswater

One of the most popular walks in the Lake District is undoubtedly along the south-eastern side of Ullswater. A great day out usually begins with taking the steamboat to Howtown and then following the path along the shore back to Glenridding. There are some superb views on this walk looking up to the head of the lake, but I think the finest vista is looking across the lake beyond these magnificent pines.

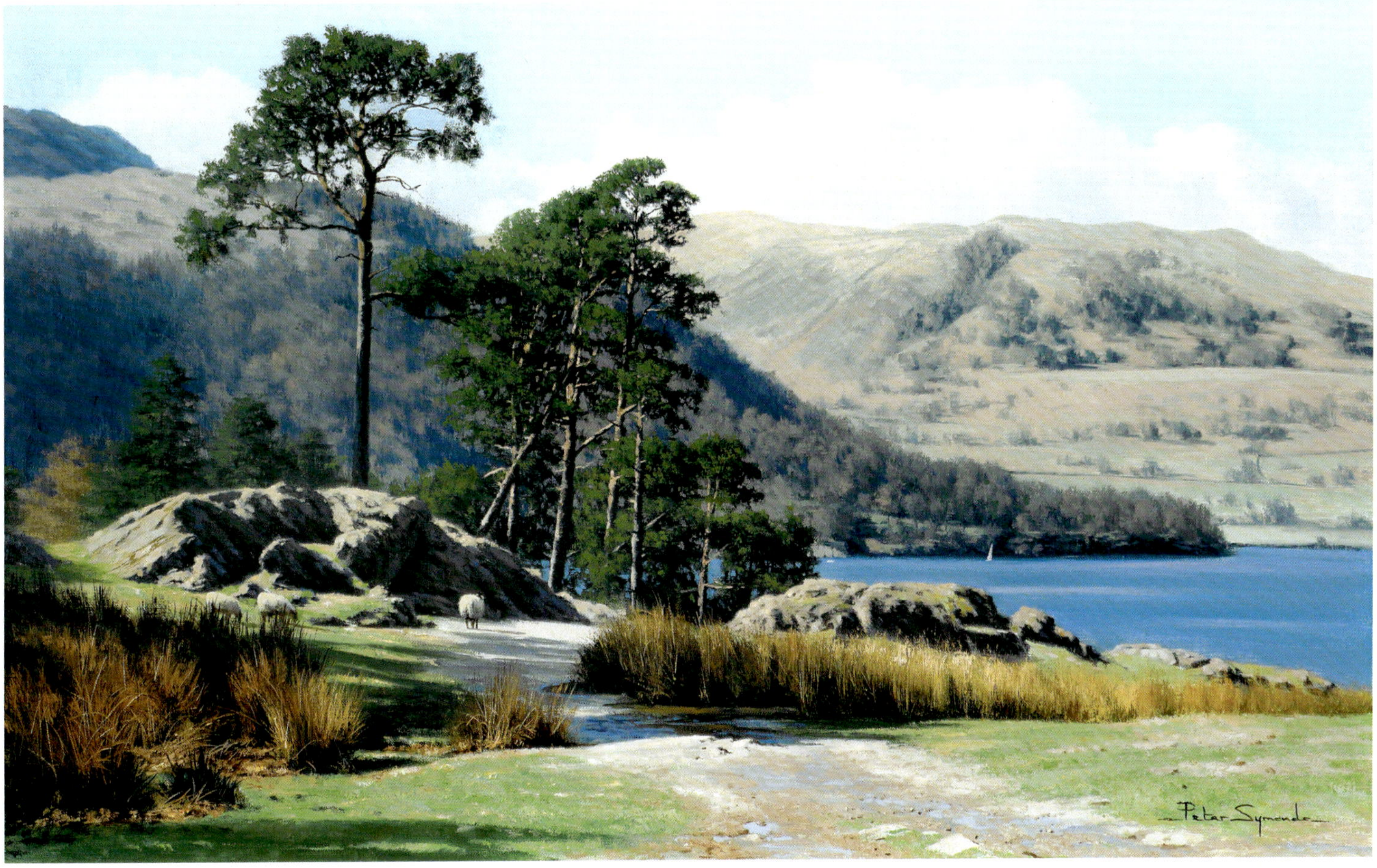
Peter Symonds

Fleetwith Pike from Crummock Water

At the south-western end of Crummock Water, one leaves the confines of Mellbreak's slopes for a large open area of grassland and trees (although it can frequently be damp underfoot). I love the views up to Fleetwith Pike from here, particularly when a lack of wind allows the fells to mirror themselves in the water.

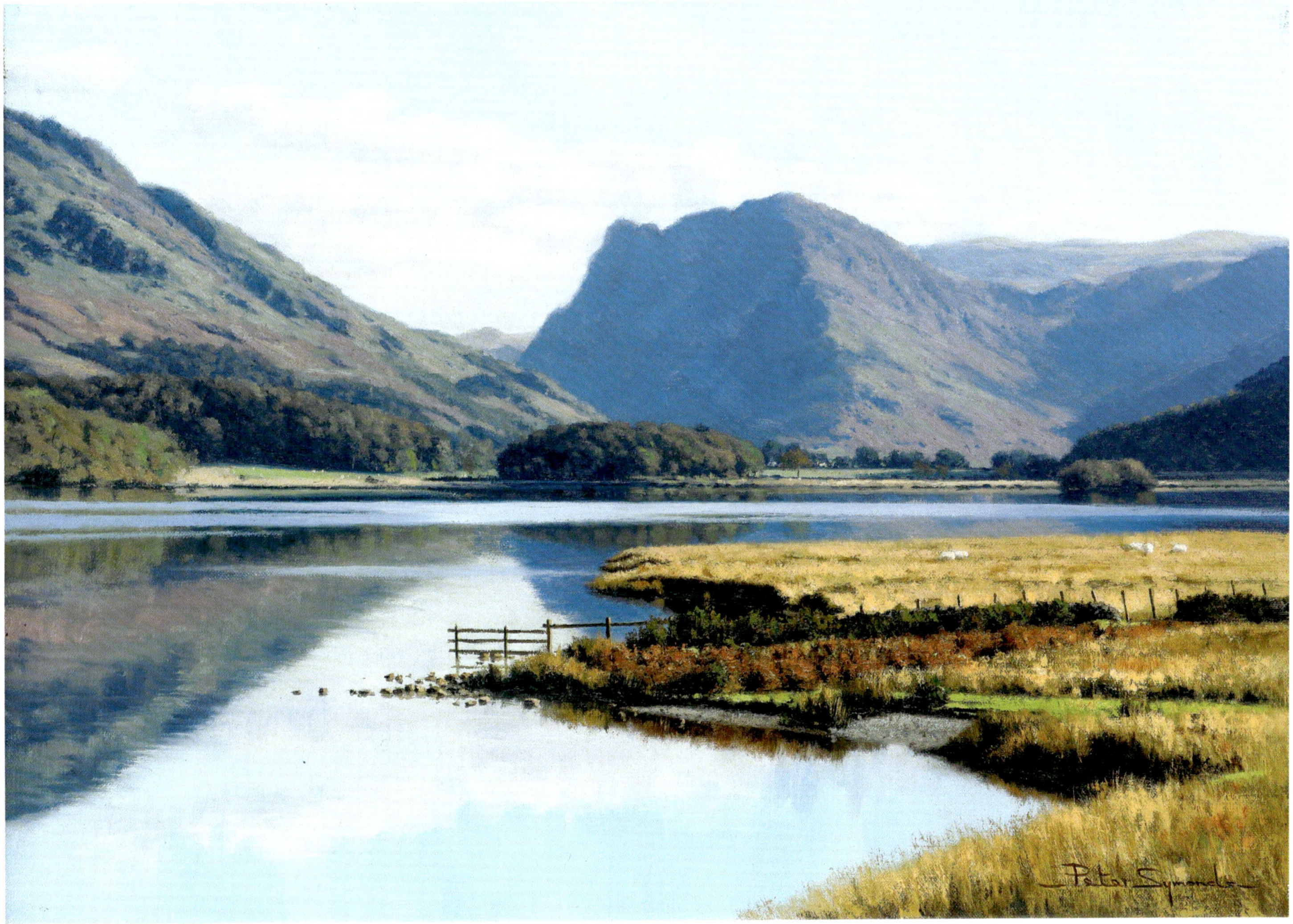
Peter Symonds

Beside the Beck, High Rannerdale

Tucked in between Rannerdale Knotts and Whiteless Pike, this has to be one of the shortest valleys in the Lakes, a little more than a mile in length. This picture was always going to be quite a challenge to paint because of the riot of autumnal colour. Bringing the foreground into shadow partly solved the problem, but keeping some of the values more muted hopefully prevented the viewer from being bombarded by too many competing colours.

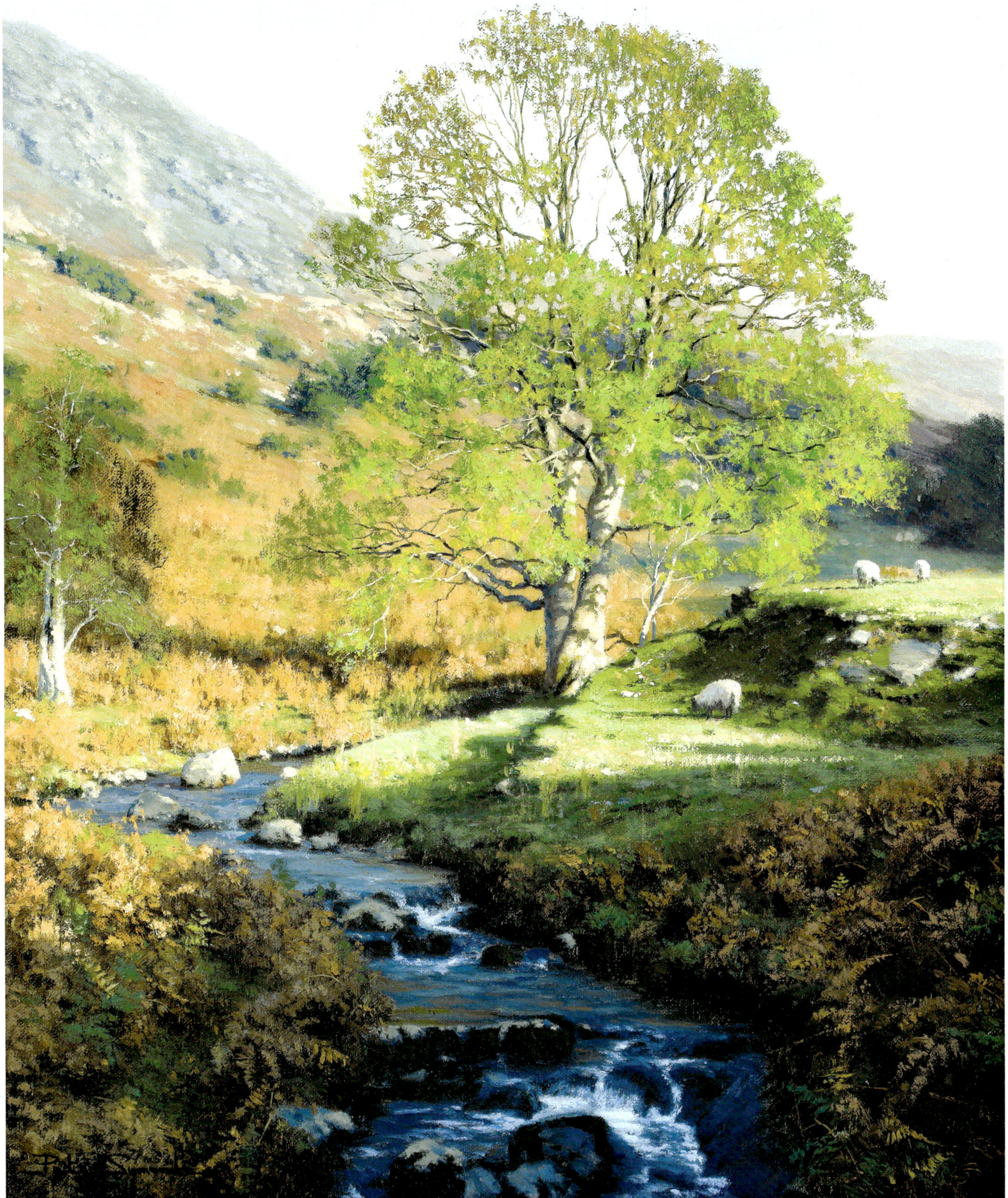

Late Afternoon, Buttermere

There had to be one painting in the book of this striking view of Fleetwith Pike from the shores of Buttermere. The walk around this stunning lake is only about four and a half miles and there are fine views of the high fells that surround it, but its popularity with walkers can make it very busy at times.

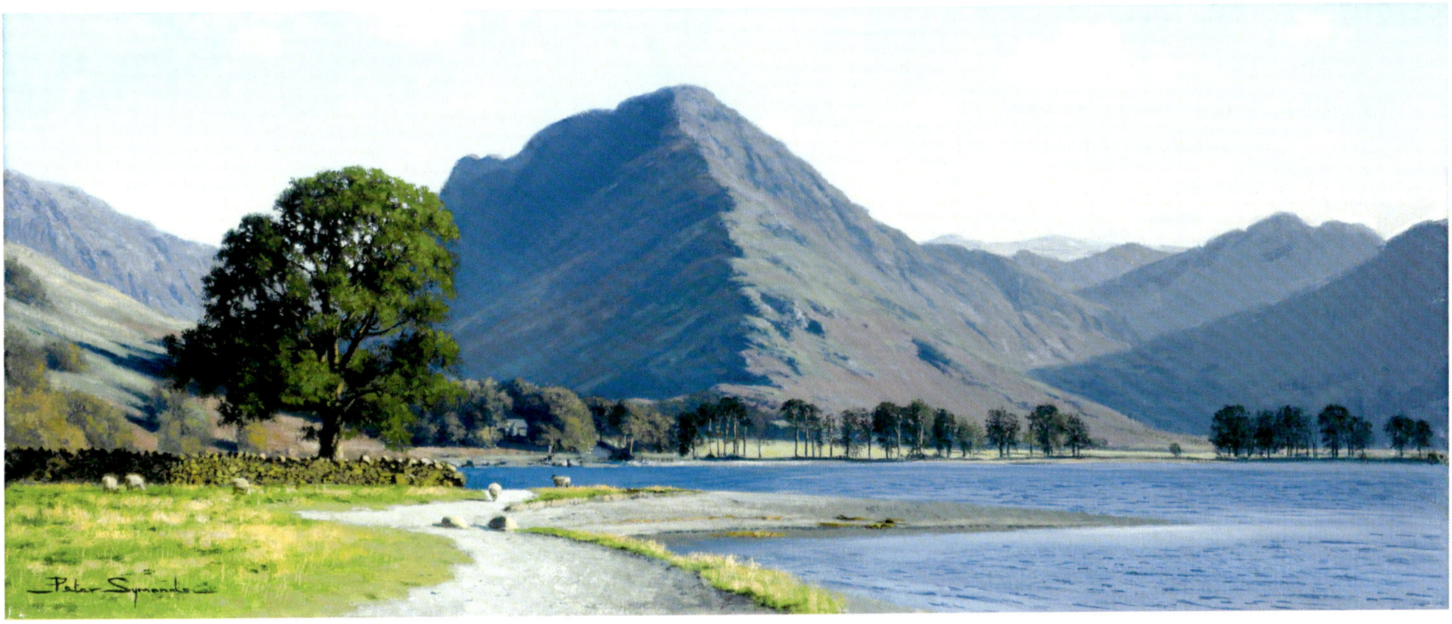
Peter Symonds

An October Afternoon, Martindale

The valleys to the east of Ullswater are quiet and crowd-free, and I hesitated momentarily before advertising their beauty for fear of diminishing their tranquillity in any way. There are some beautiful becks that flow down from the hills here. I think these dales look their best in the autumn and winter months when the all-pervading greenery has left the fells and the reeds and grasses turn to many shades of gold.

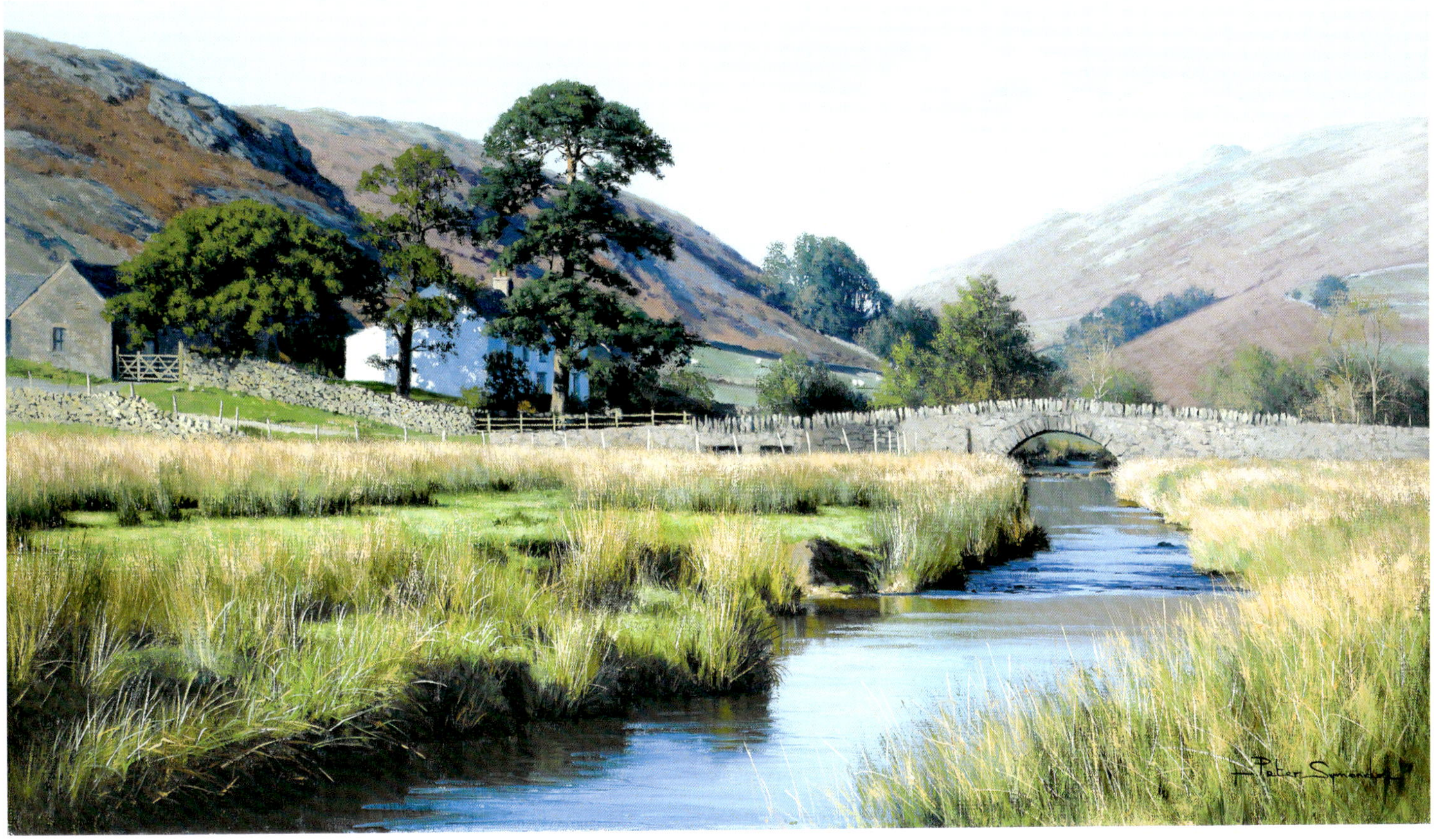

Local Traffic, Boredale near Ullswater

Very rarely do sheep just appear in the right place at the right time, and any effort to gently herd them to the right spot usually results in them disappearing in the other direction. This little group, however, were very obliging, and for once did not seem to panic – thus allowing me to take a quick photo of them in situ before they carried on to the fields beyond.

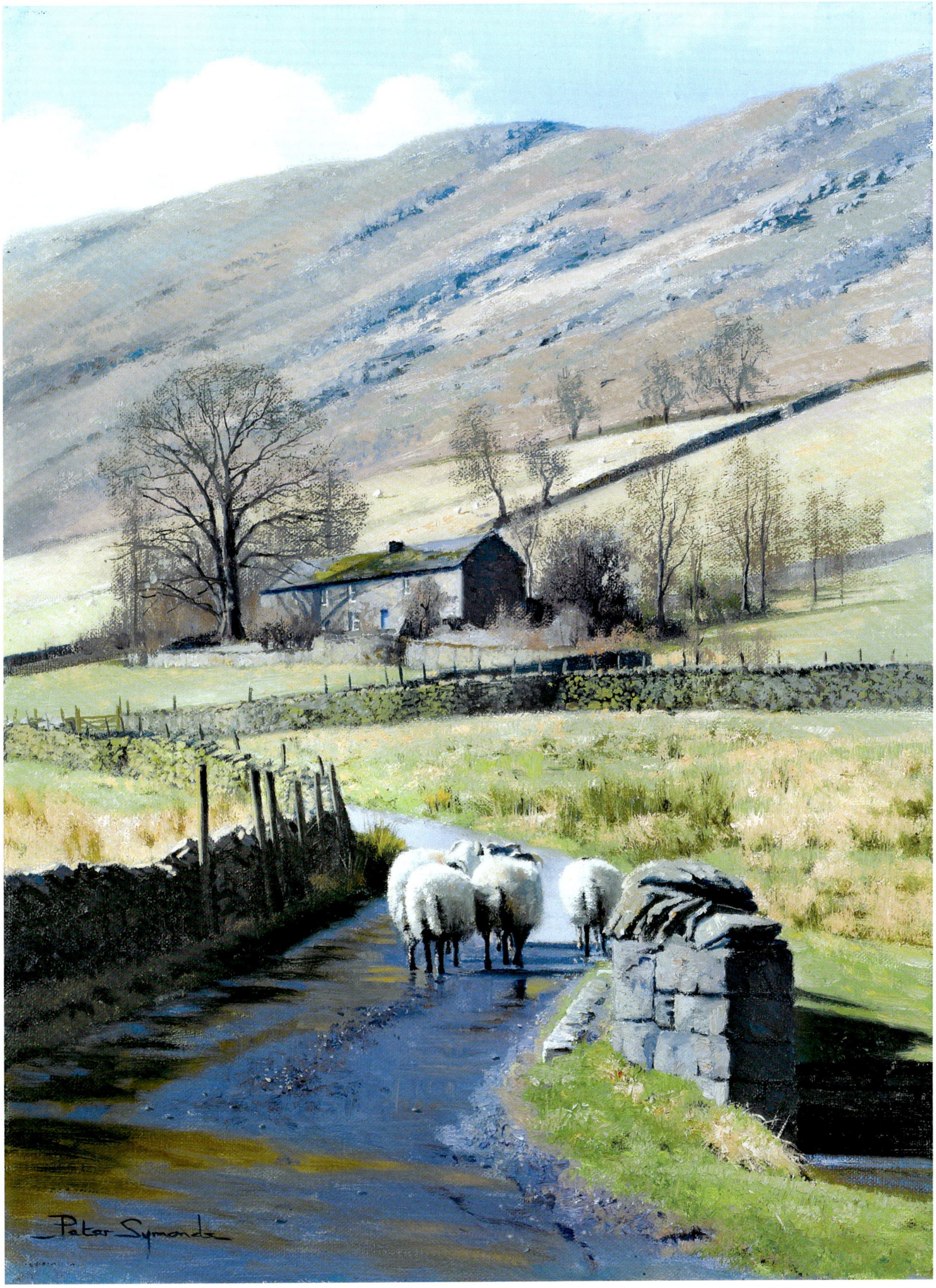
Peter Symonds

Allen Crags and Esk Pike from Sprinkling Crag Tarn

Sprinkling Tarn is well known to all who have walked up to Esk Hause from Sty Head. Much less visited, as it lies a few hundred yards to the north and off the main path, is this delightful tarn, unnamed on the map but usually referred to as Sprinkling Crag Tarn.

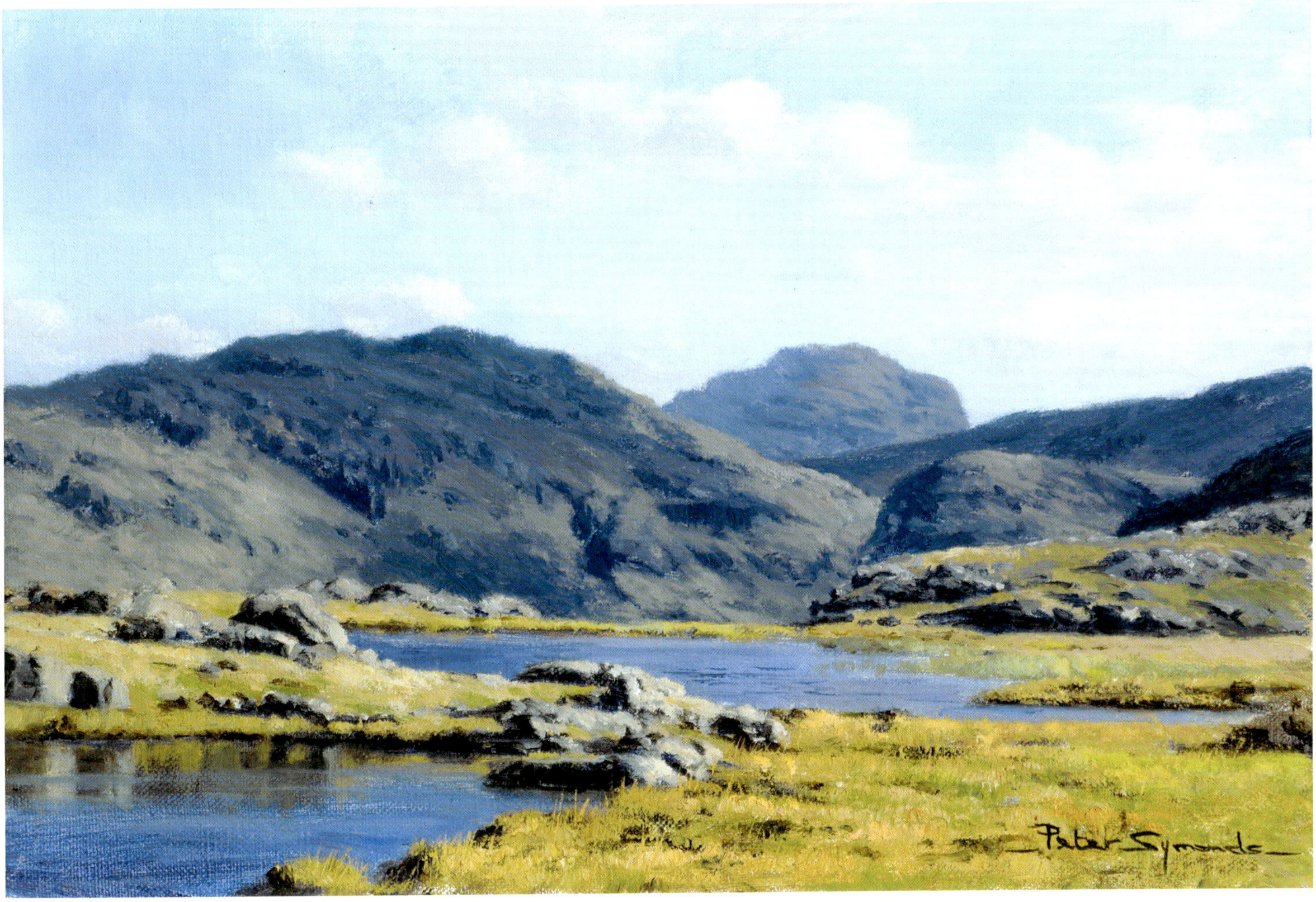
Peter Symonds

Frosty Morning at Manesty, Grange-in-Borrowdale

A postman in Borrowdale once told me that the early hours on his route were often the sunniest time of day in the Lakes, and I have often found this to be true. On this particular morning there was not only a beautiful sunrise, but a lovely mist that hung in the valley for an hour or so. The early bird does often catch the worm!

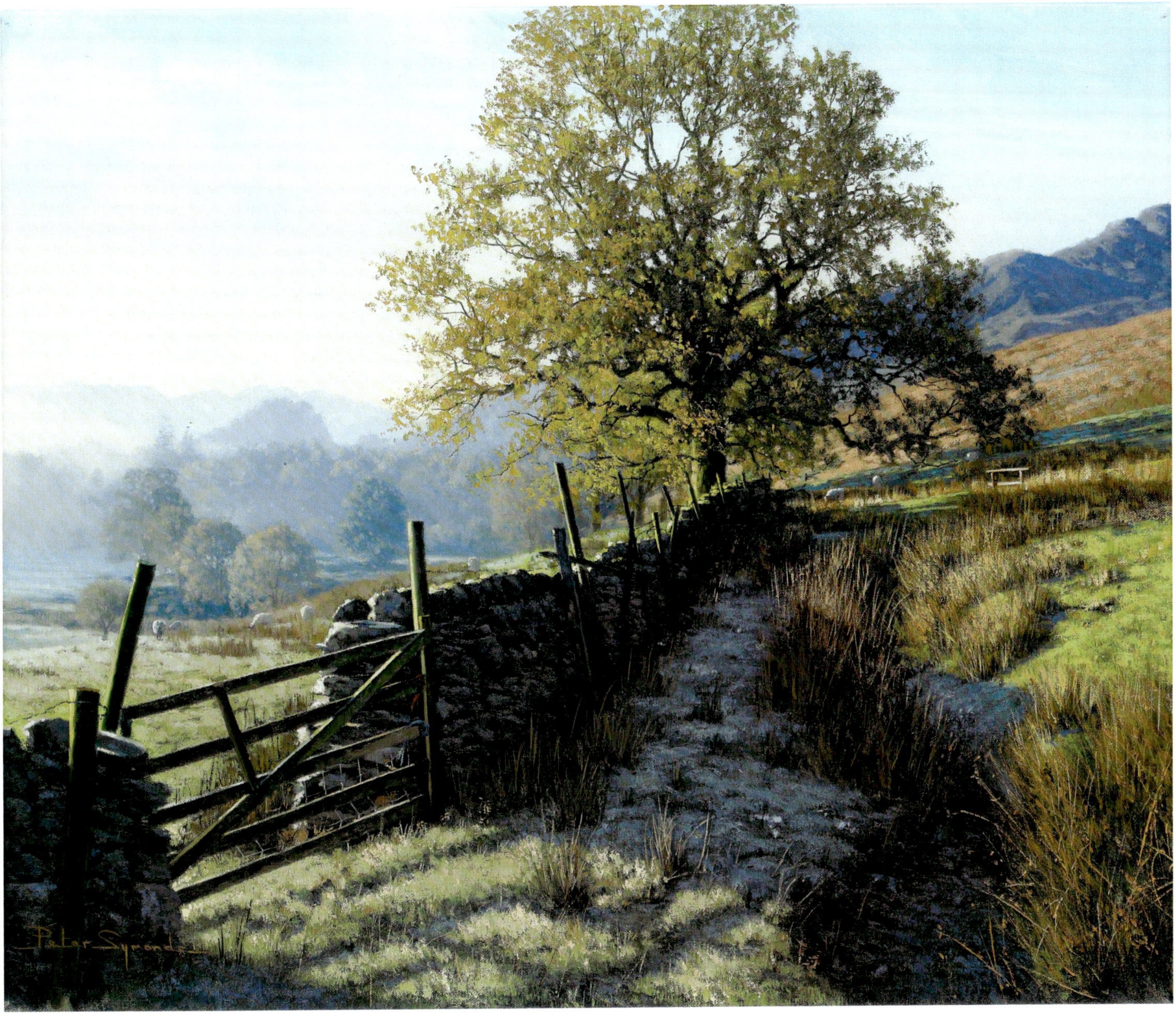

Early Autumn, Boredale near Ullswater

This is a beautiful place that I love to visit whenever I go around to the back of Ullswater, and my children love to paddle about in the stream here and build dams. So do I – but only with them around!

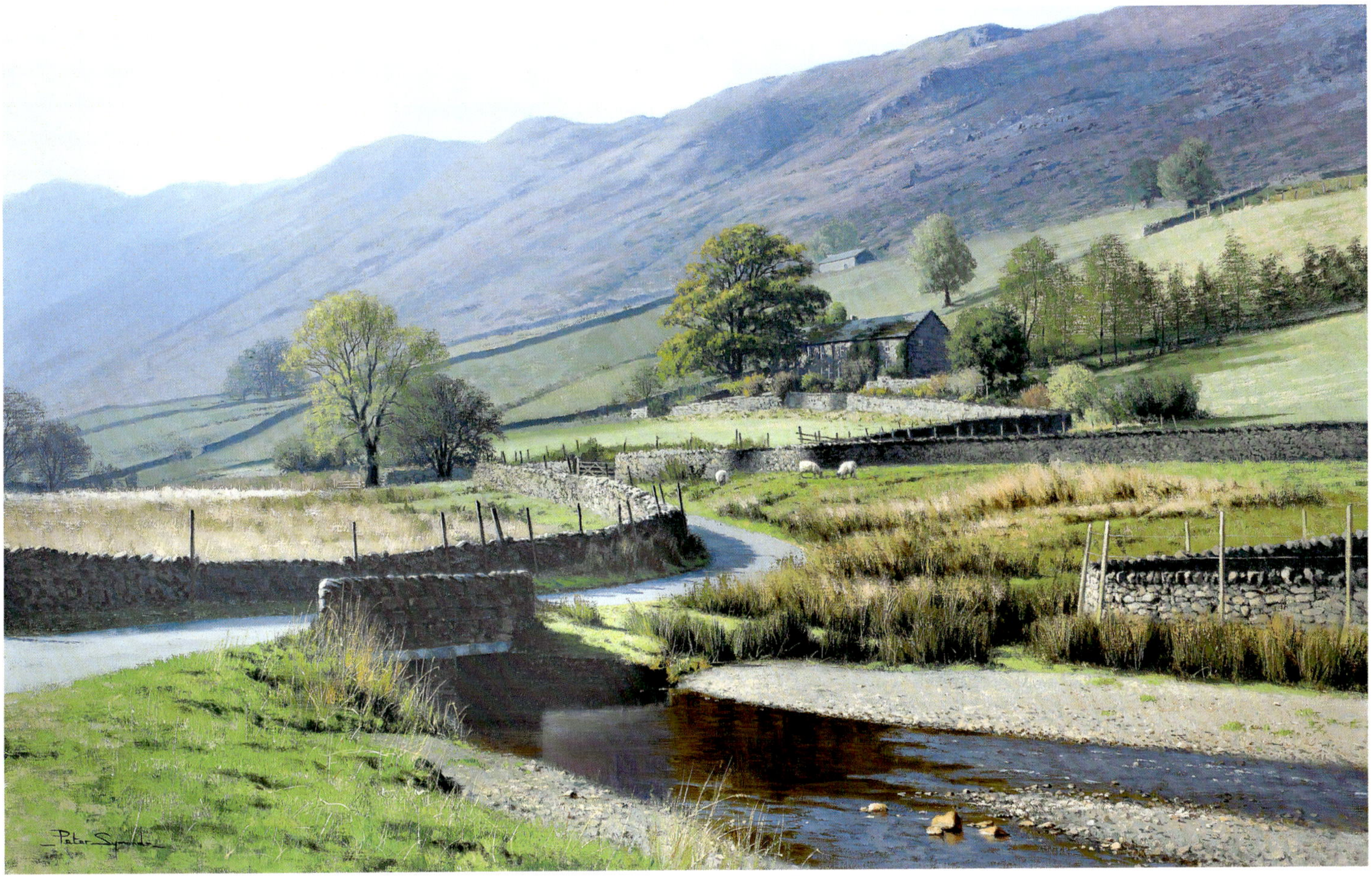

A Bright October Day, Buttermere

There are endless scenes to paint around Buttermere, which for many is the most beautiful lake in the National Park. It is a very popular subject with artists and I am always intrigued by how others see and then interpret the scenes that they choose to paint. If one was to set a dozen painters in front of a location at the same time, it would be fascinating to see just how differently each one would tackle the same theme. There should be a glorious freedom for the artist to interpret the subject just as he or she wants to, rather than merely recording it as a camera would.

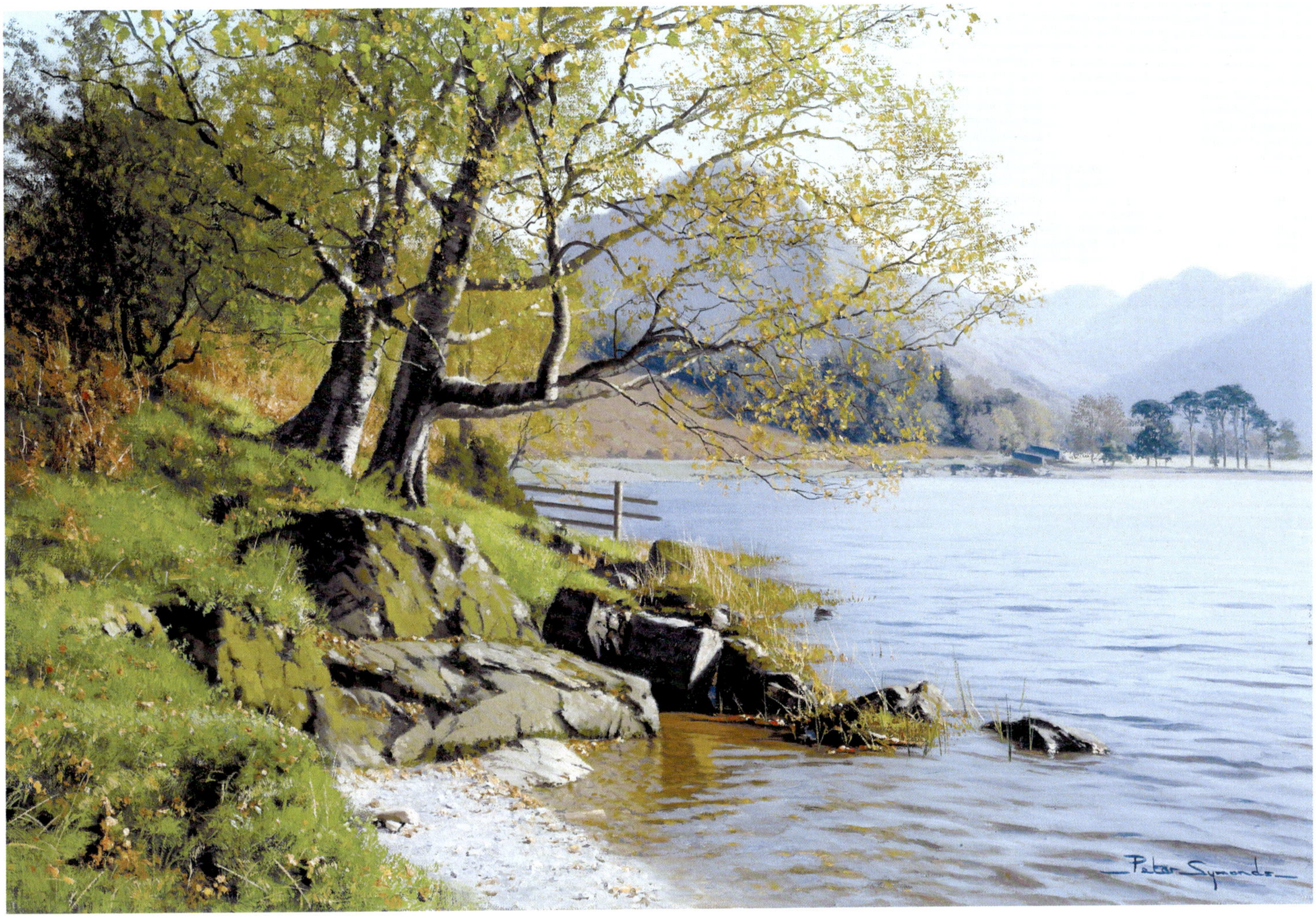
Peter Symonds

Autumn, near Stonethwaite, Borrowdale

When I first started to paint over twenty-five years ago, a favourite subject of mine was often large, solitary trees standing amongst the fields and hedgerows of Surrey and Sussex. When first exploring the Lake District I always felt the trees here to be grander and shapelier, and still feel this to be true, although I have yet to reason as to why this should be so.

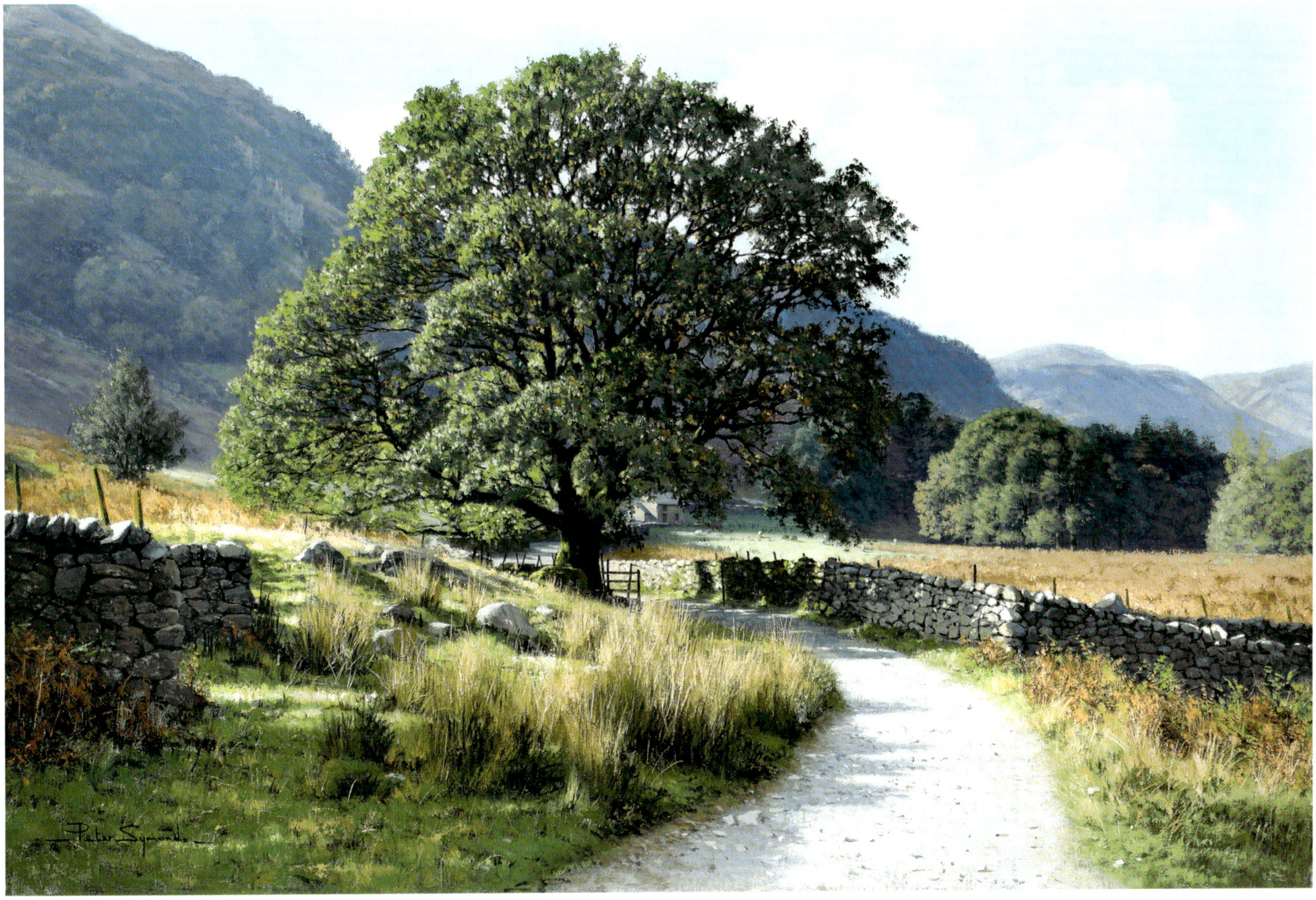

Path to Grisedale Tarn

When walking in the Lake District many people would say the greatest joy is getting to the top of a fell, a pass or even a tarn. I would have to agree, but there is also a similar delight at the start or during the walk-in when all the yet unknown sights and experiences of the day still lie ahead. I have often felt that anticipation when setting off up Grisedale, particularly on a morning such as the one depicted here when the morning rain and clouds start to leave the tops.

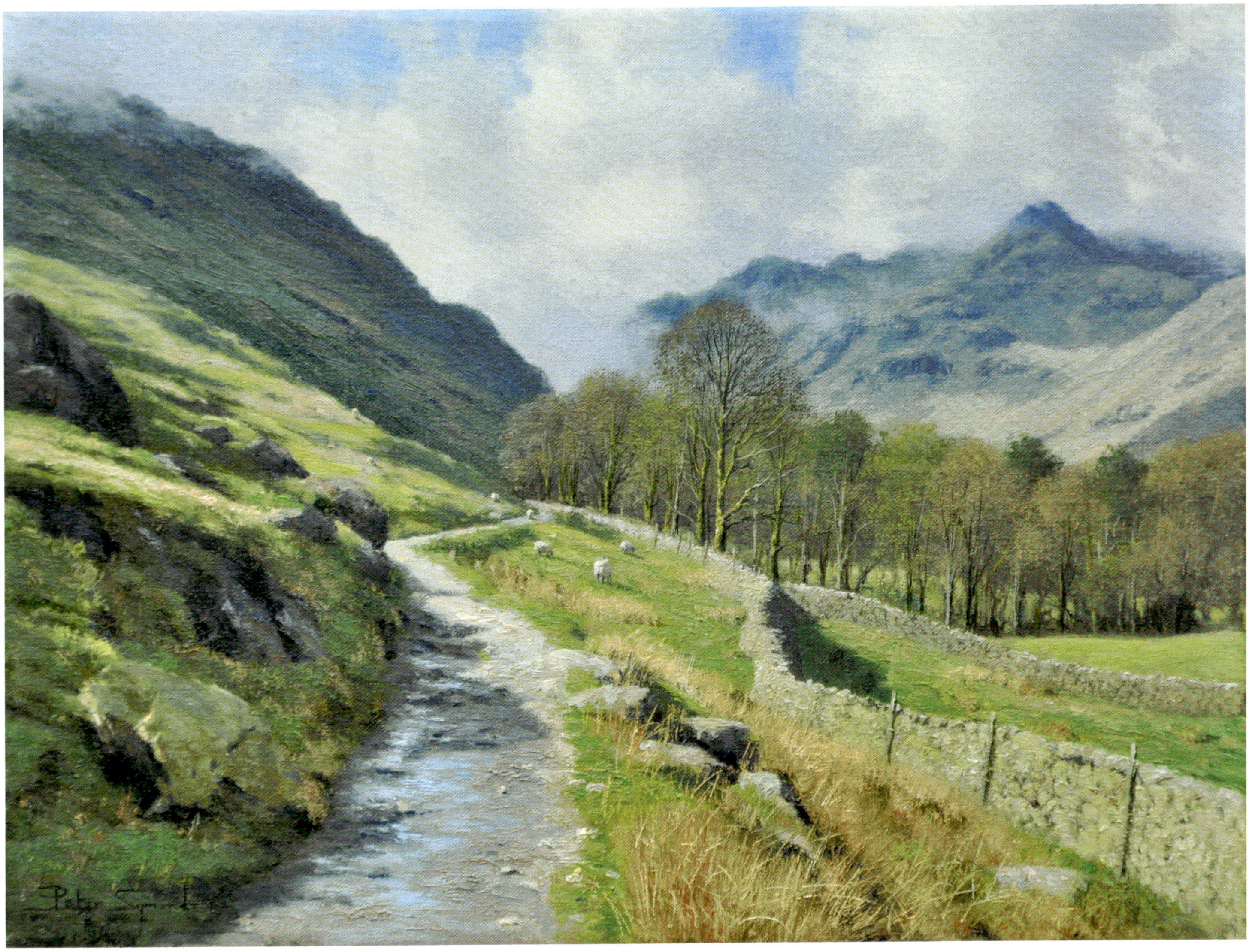

A Winter Afternoon, Martindale

Many artists would agree that the best atmospheric effects occur when they paint facing the light, known as painting "a contre jour". It helps by simplifying the shadows and half-tones while enabling the light accents to 'sing' more powerfully.

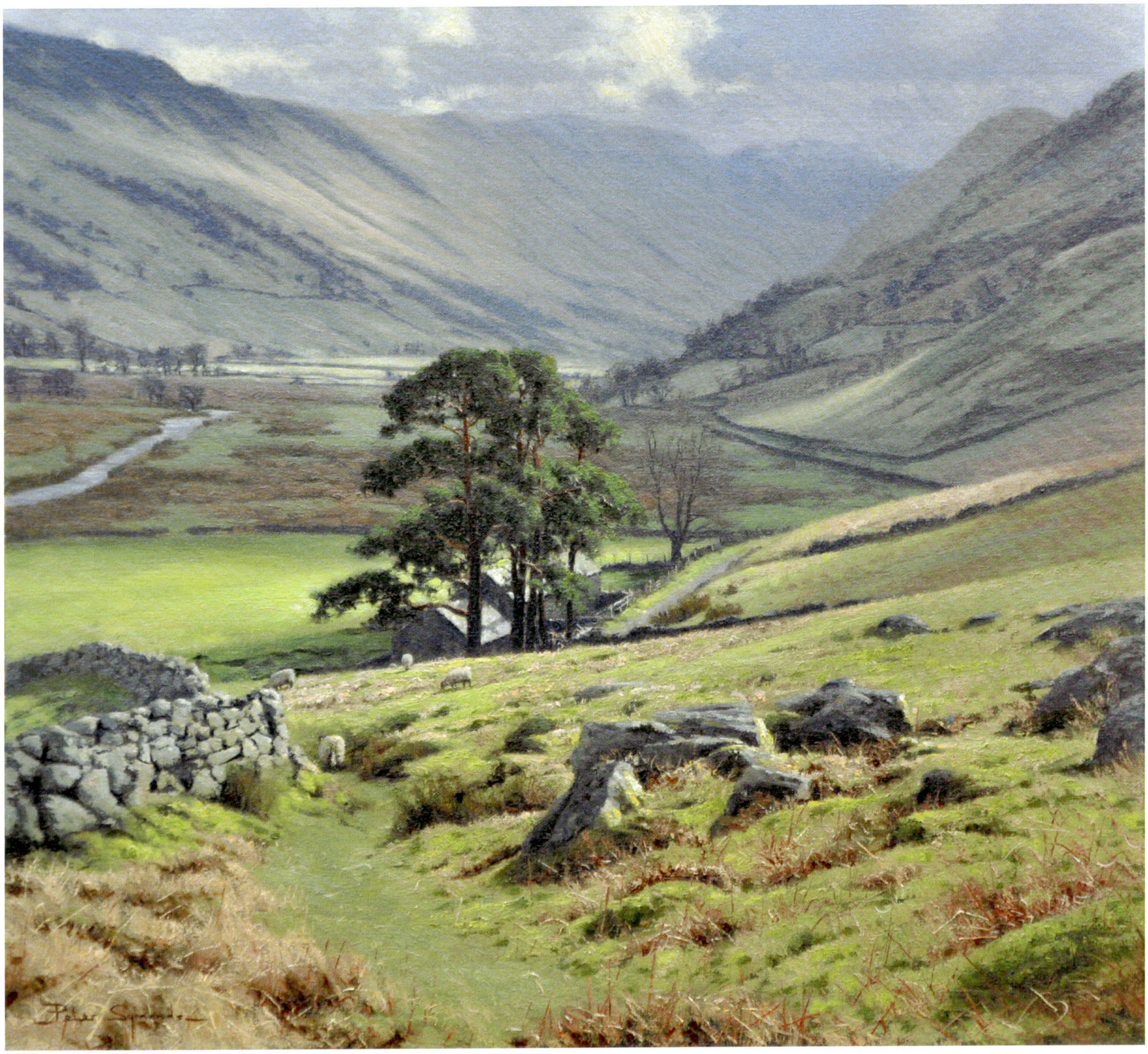

River Brathay near Elterwater

The drive west from Ambleside towards the Langdales offers many tantalising glimpses of the River Brathay and I rarely resist the chance to pop down to the river at a spot just south of Elterwater. There are views to paint in all directions from here.

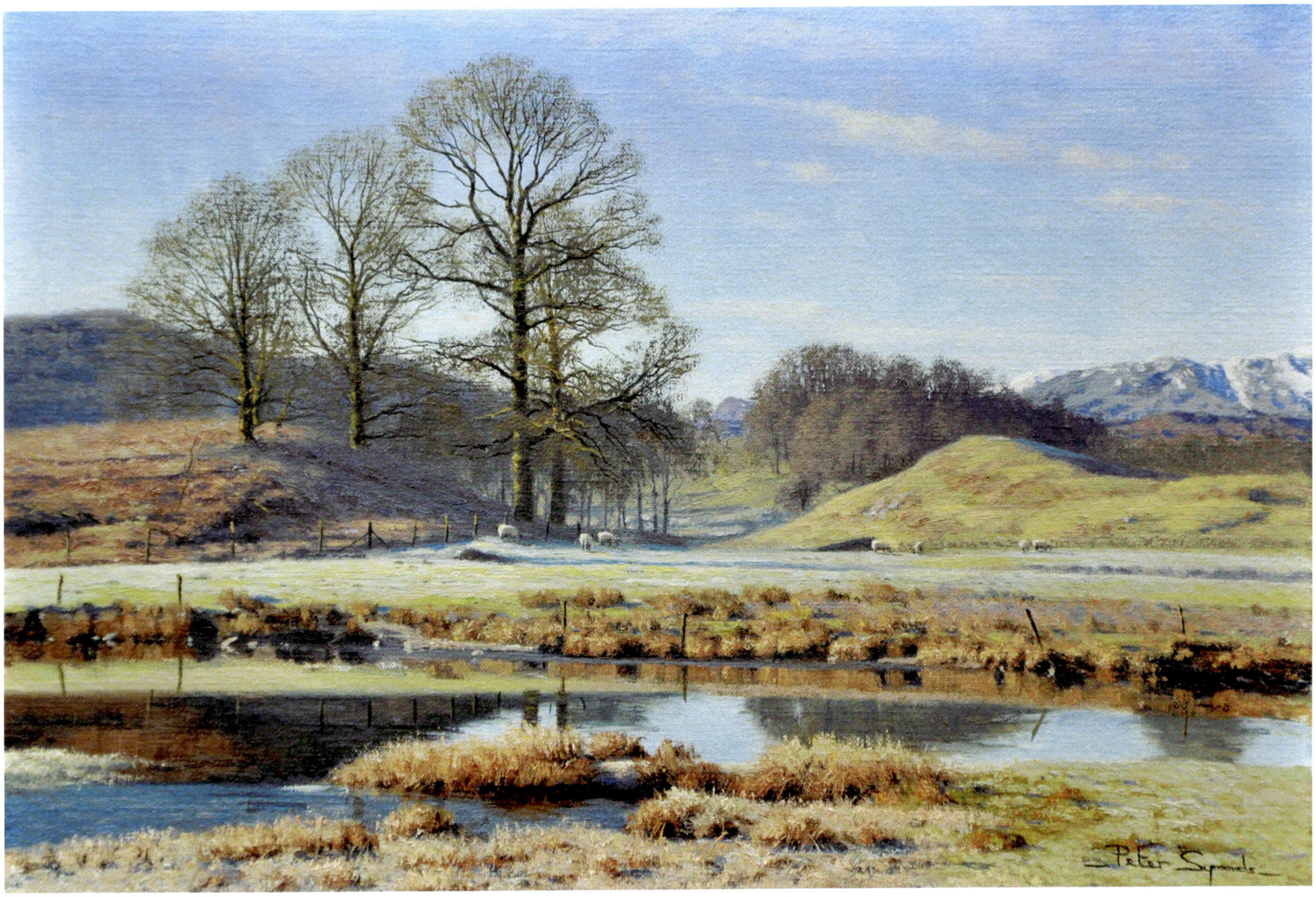

Walking the Dog, Troutbeck

Troutbeck is a gem of a village and in my opinion is the most picturesque in the Lake District.

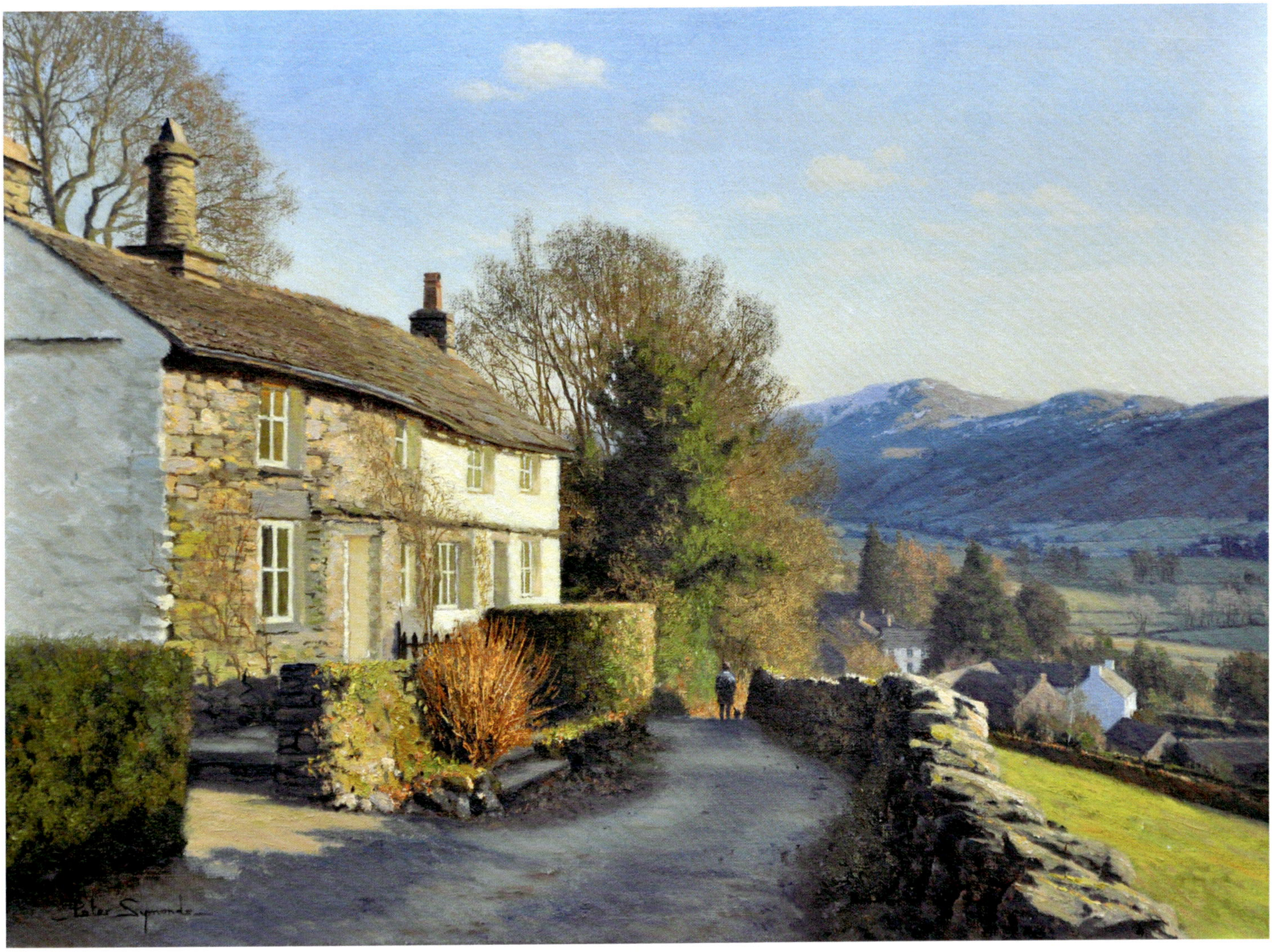

Autumn Skies, Greenburn

One of the many reasons I love to paint in the Lake District is the beautiful skies that so often occur here. Any landscape painter knows that the sky is the key to setting the atmosphere of a painting and big cloud formations such as these can give real drama to a scene.

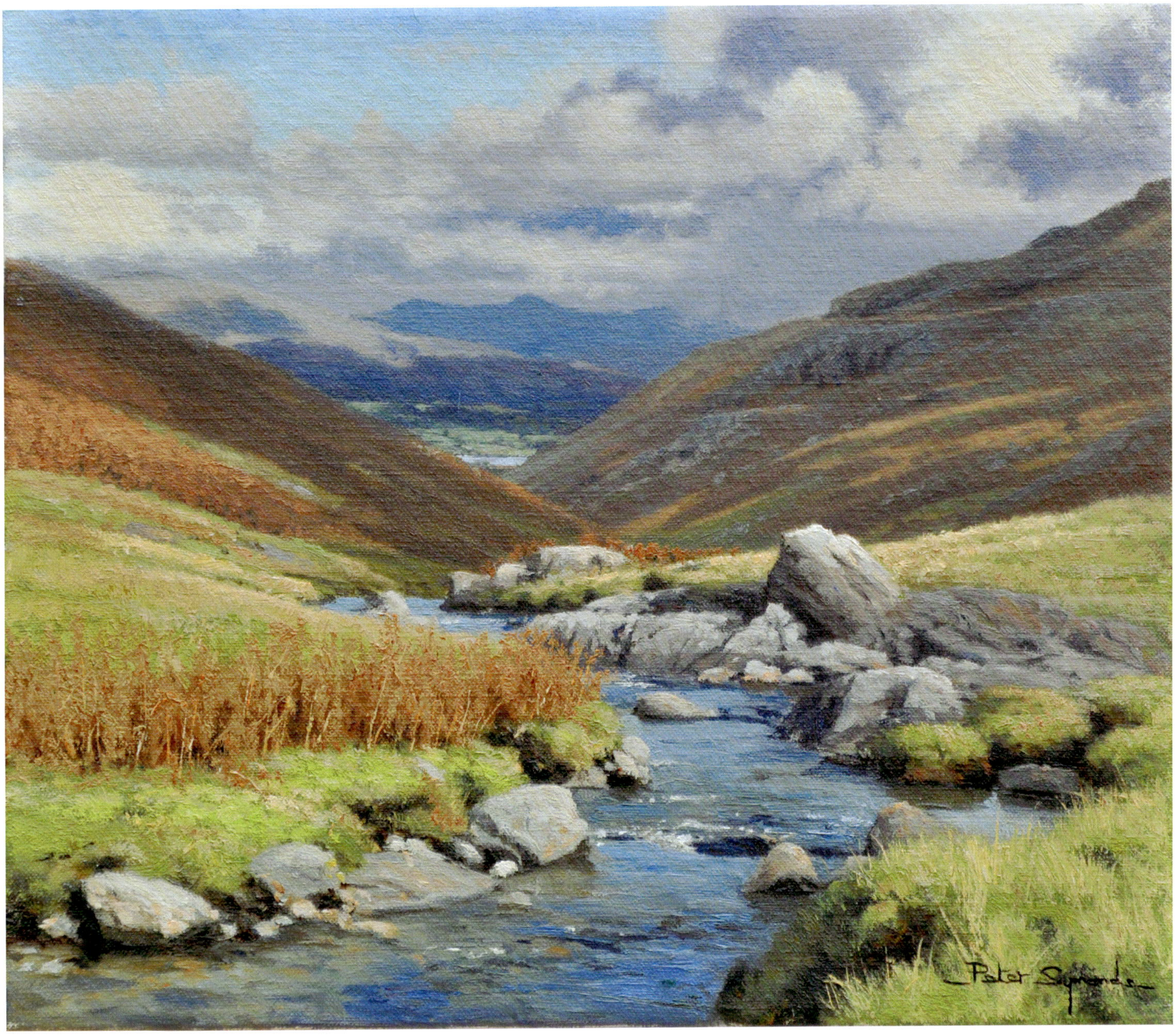
Peter Symonds

Langdale Pikes from Blea Tarn

Most painters and photographers move onto a place by the shore to capture this scene, partly because there is a nice grouping of trees that can then be incorporated. Personally, I prefer to view the tarn from a little higher up as the foreground makes for a better approach into the painting.

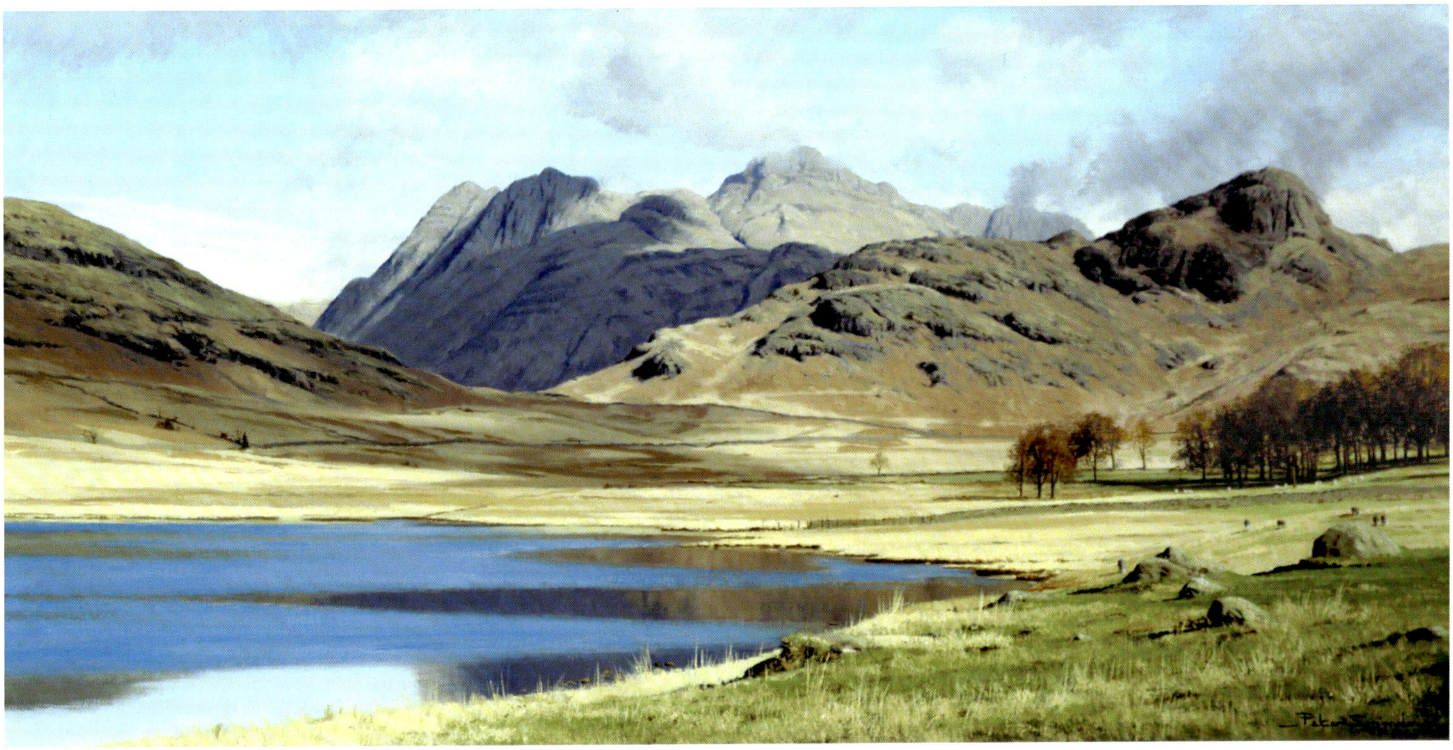

Days End Wastwater

The Lake District National Park has used this view looking up Wastwater as the basis for its logo since 1951. It was also voted Britain's favourite view by ITV in 2008. Need one say anymore?!

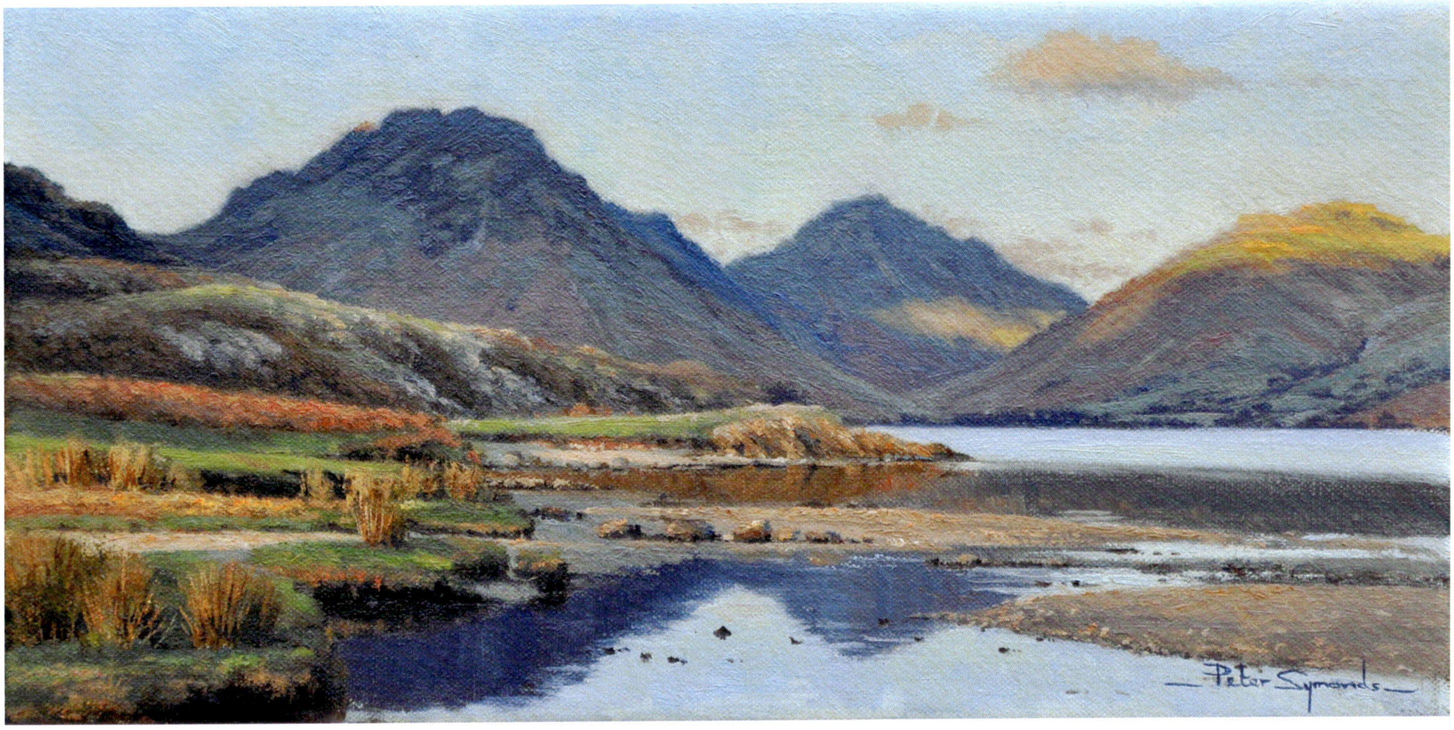
Peter Symonds

Wastwater Screes from Greendale

The imposing scree slopes along Wastwater are normally painted and photographed from the lakeshore, but in the evening light they made a great backdrop to this more pastoral scene.

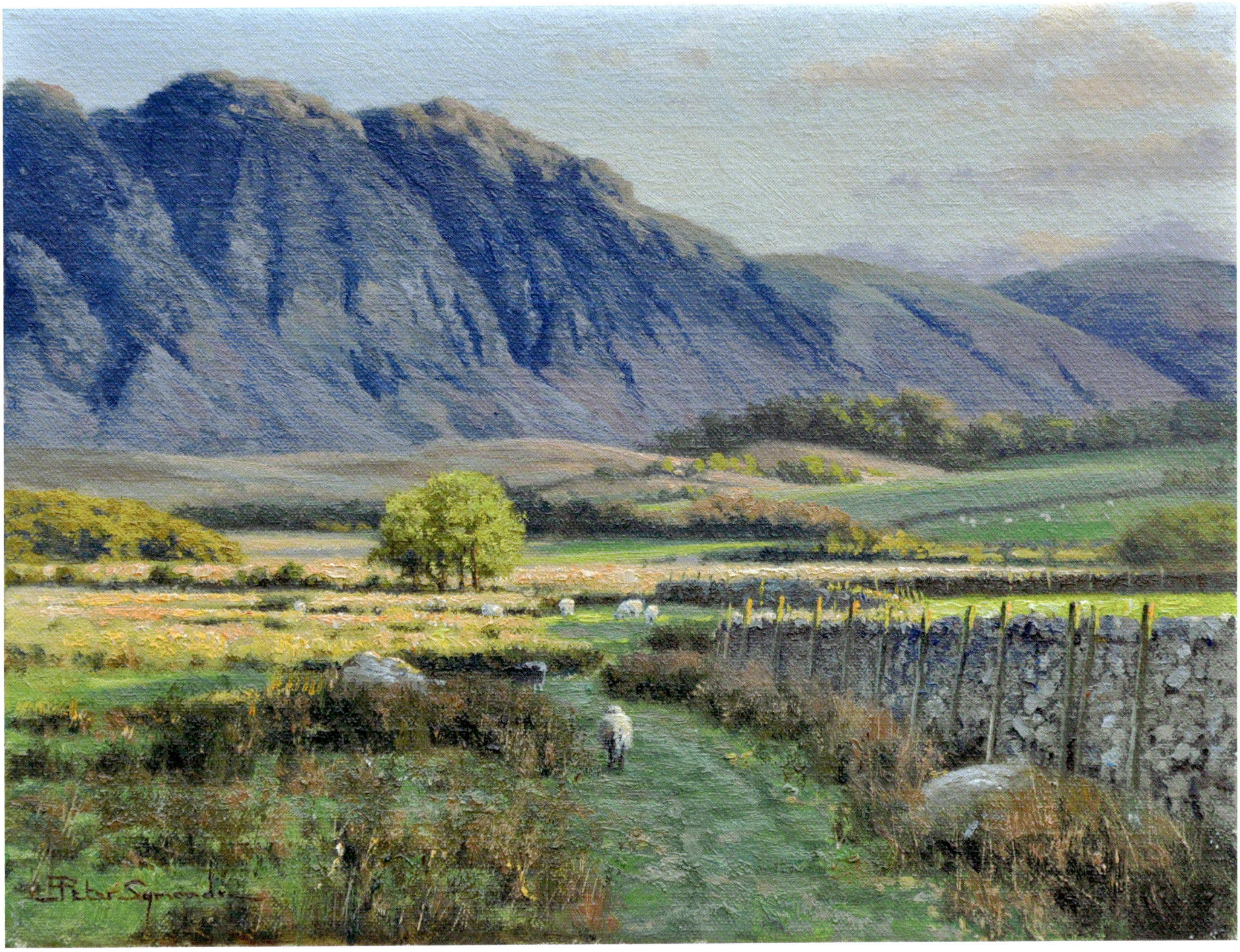

Frosty Morning, River Brathay

Early starts often provide wonderful lighting on the landscape, but on bitterly cold winter mornings there is always the difficulty of depicting the foreground fields under heavy frost.

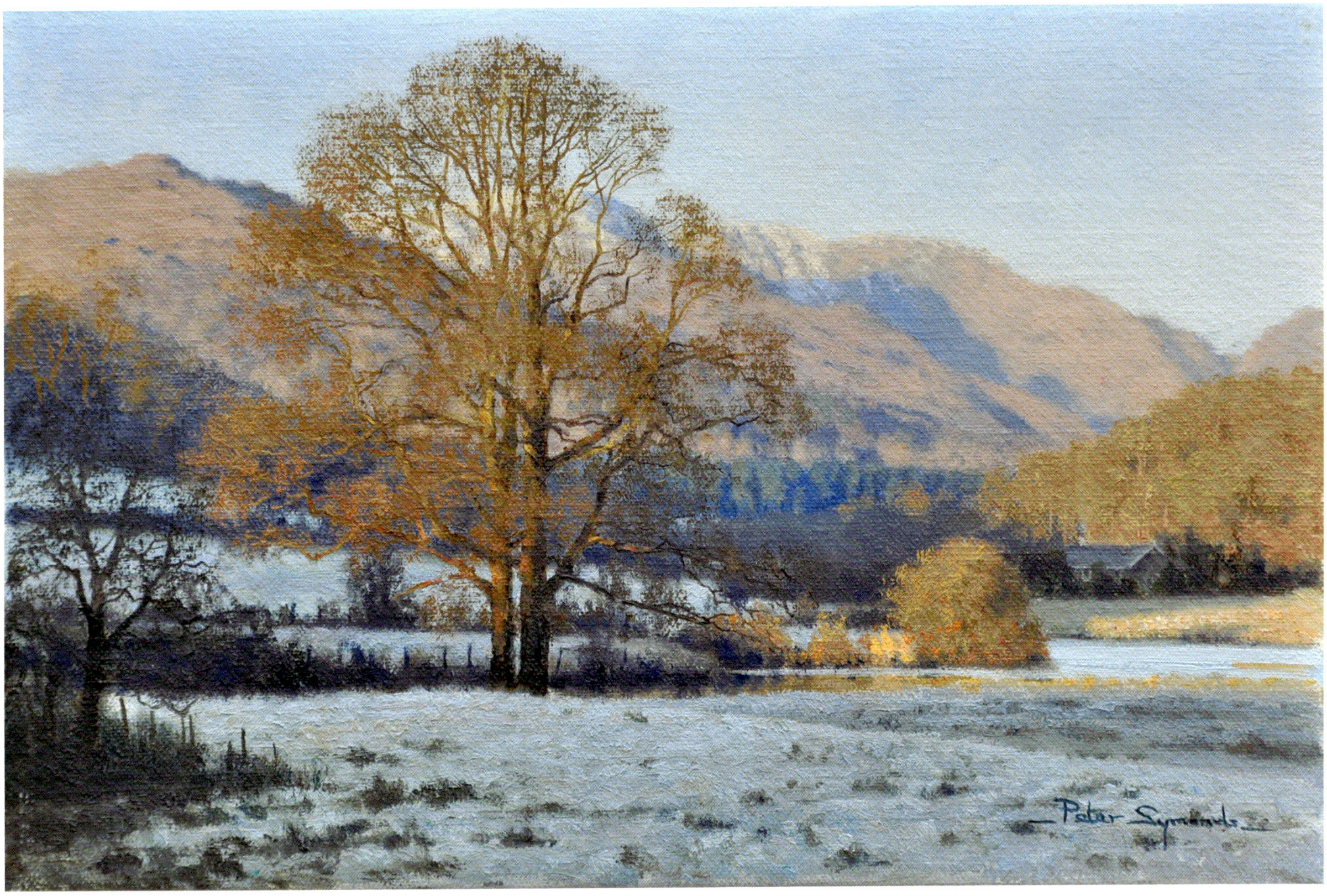
Peter Symonds

Dawn, Derwentwater

One of the great attractions for the visitor to the Lakes is having unrestricted access to such a large part of the National Park. There are relatively few areas where privately-owned land denies the walker this privilege, and that thankfully includes access to much of the main lakes. As in so many other places around the world it could have easily been the case that lavish hotels and expensive private residences grabbed prime lakeshore locations. This would have left so many of us unable to enjoy views such as this scene by Derwentwater looking over to Causey Pike.

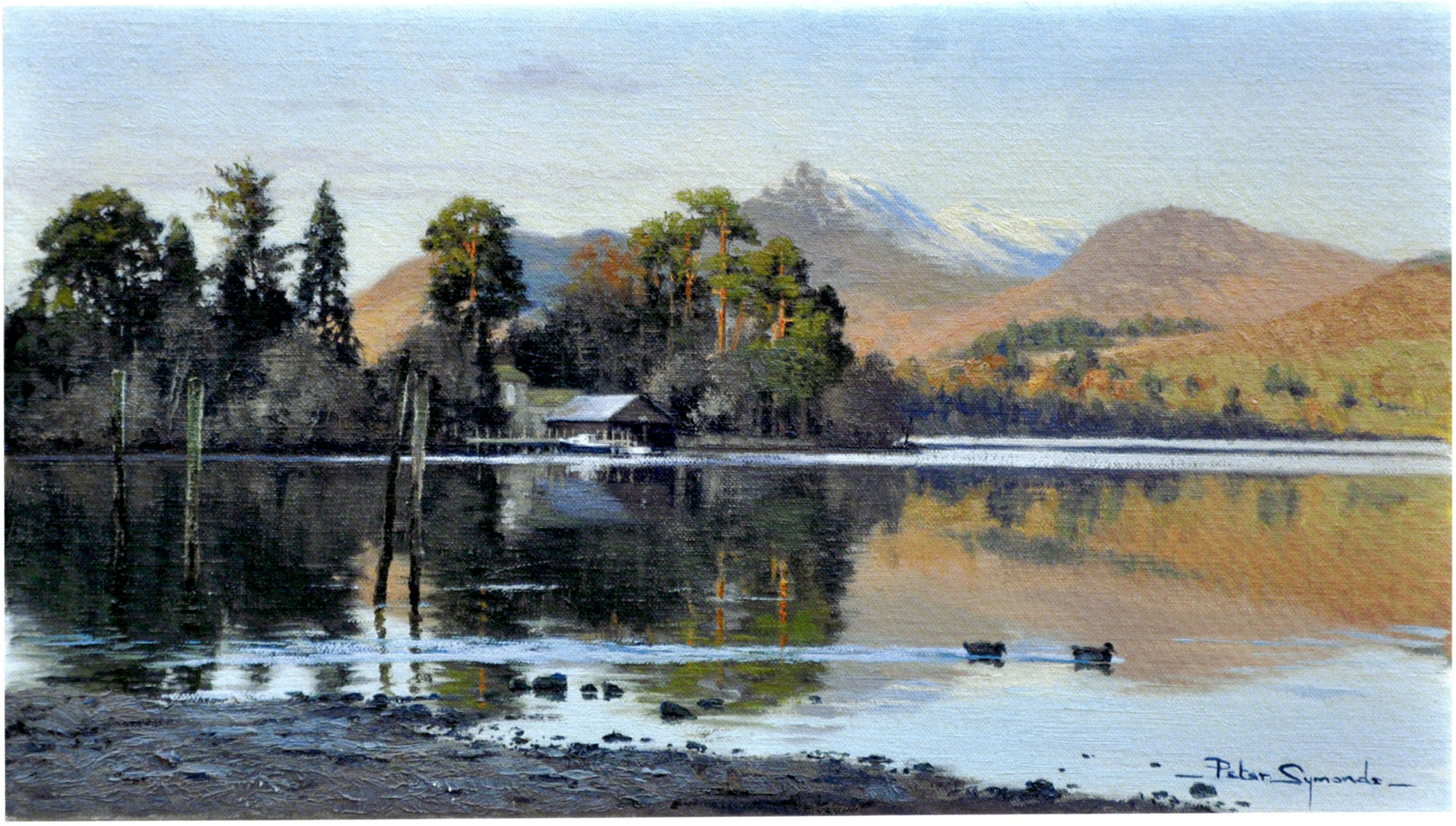
Peter Symonds

Catstycam and Glenridding Beck

One of the deservedly most popular walks in the Lake District is the walk up Striding Edge onto Helvellyn with a descent down Swirral Edge.
I suspect relatively few people then make the short detour up onto Catstycam before heading back to Red Tarn.

I well remember the first time I visited Catstycam several years ago on the windiest day I have ever experienced on the fells. I had to crawl onto the relatively small summit as the wind threatened to blow me over the precipitous cliffs to the north.

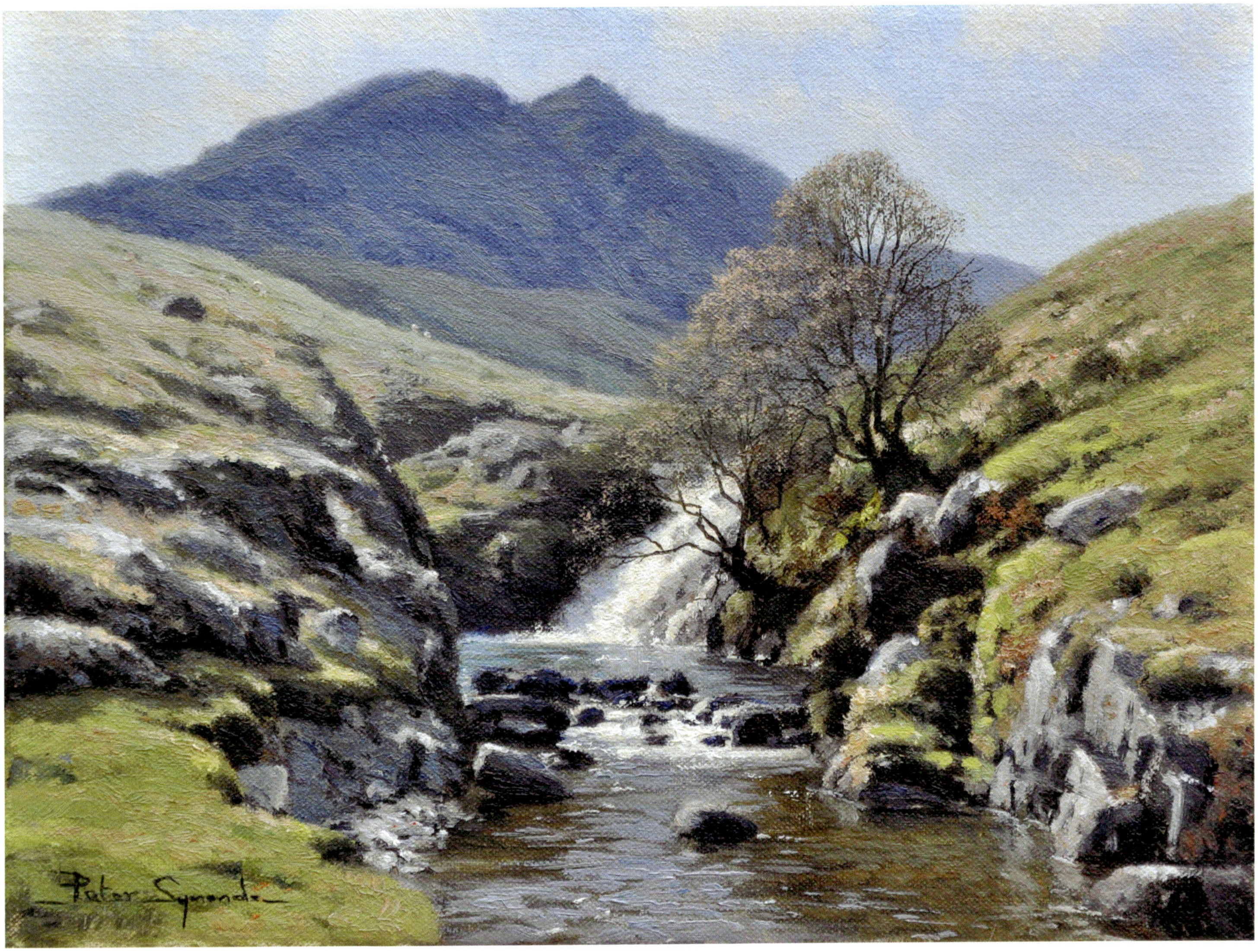
Peter Symonds

Calm Waters, Grange-in-Borrowdale

This particular view of Grange-in-Borrowdale is a gift for the painter, and my first painting of it was made into an open edition print by my publishers back in 1993 and sold many copies. It is a great shame that in recent years the shingle has been left to build up in front of the bridge here, and the river Derwent is now hardly visible from this angle, except when in spate. The bulk of the water now flows through a neighbouring bridge a few yards to the east of the picture. We stayed in the village a few years back when a great deluge of rain fell overnight, and were amazed at how high the water level had risen up the bridge. This is, after all, the river that drains the wettest place in England – Seathwaite, a few miles upstream. I, like many others, was very relieved that this beautiful bridge was not destroyed by the recent catastrophic floodwaters that did so much damage to Cockermouth further downstream.

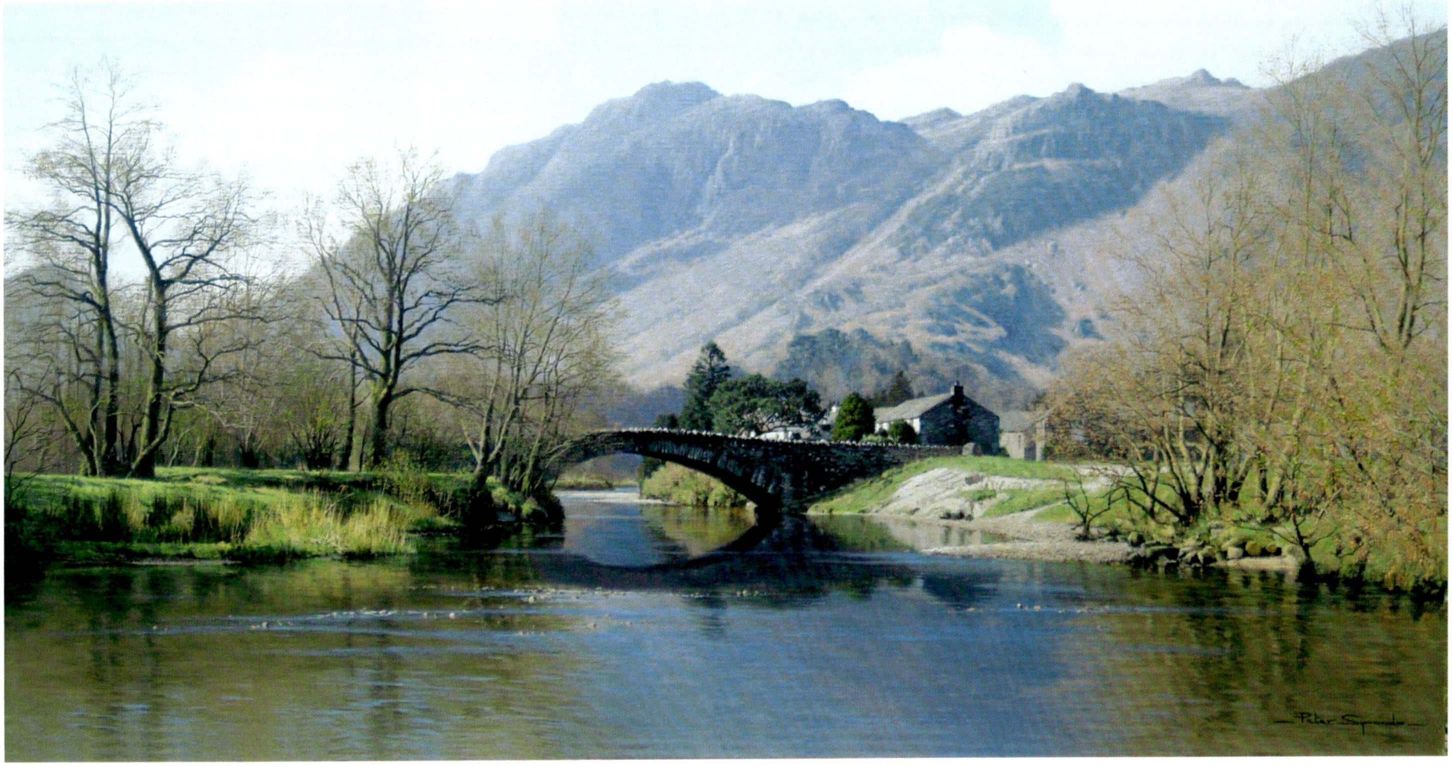

Ullswater

This is another of the wonderfully-shaped oak trees that abound in the Lake District, and can be found a short distance from Sandwick on the beautiful walk along the shores of Ullswater.

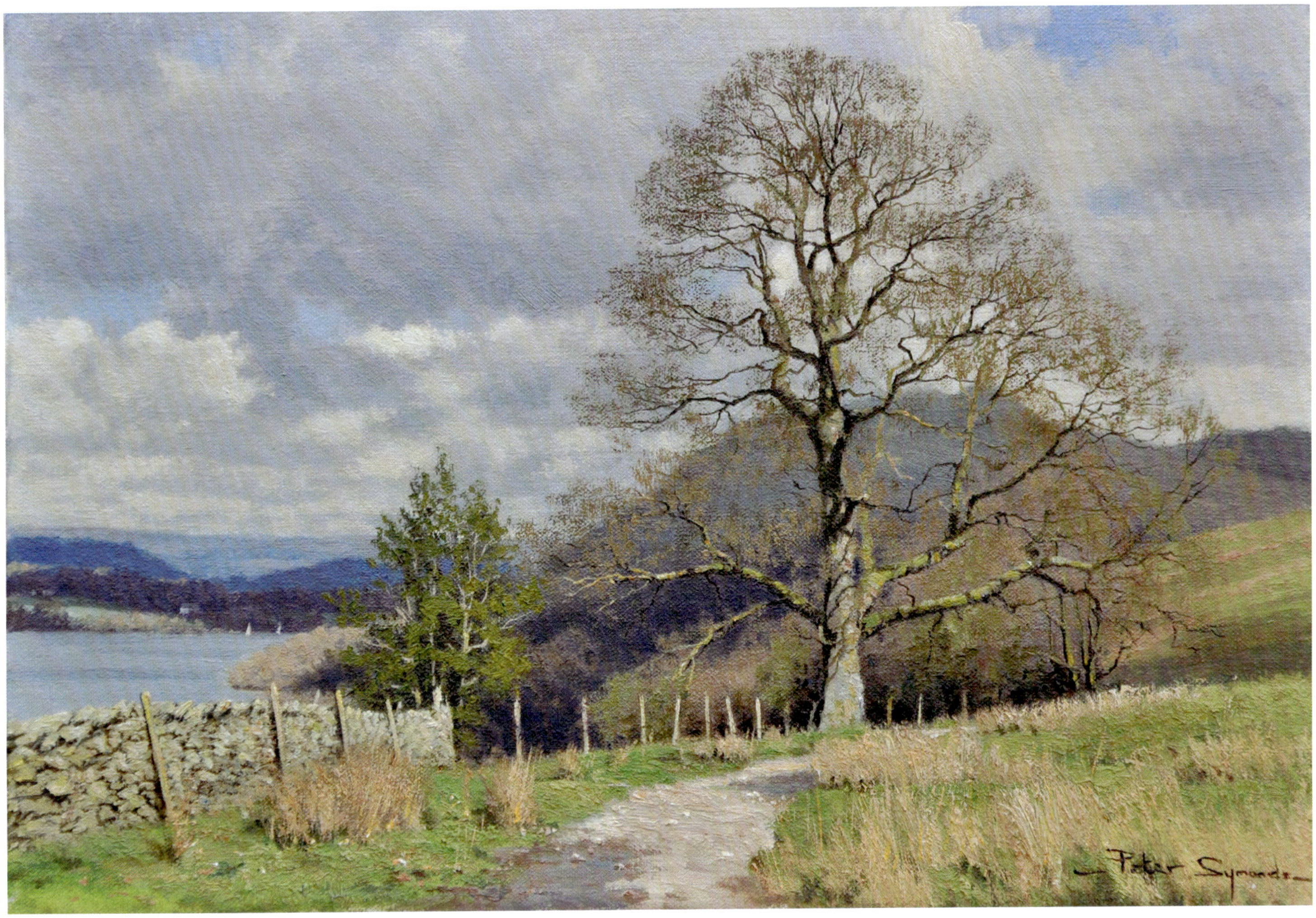
Peter Symonds

Dollywagon Pike and the Grisedale Valley

This view is well known to the hordes of walkers who each year make their way from Patterdale up to Helvellyn via Striding Edge.

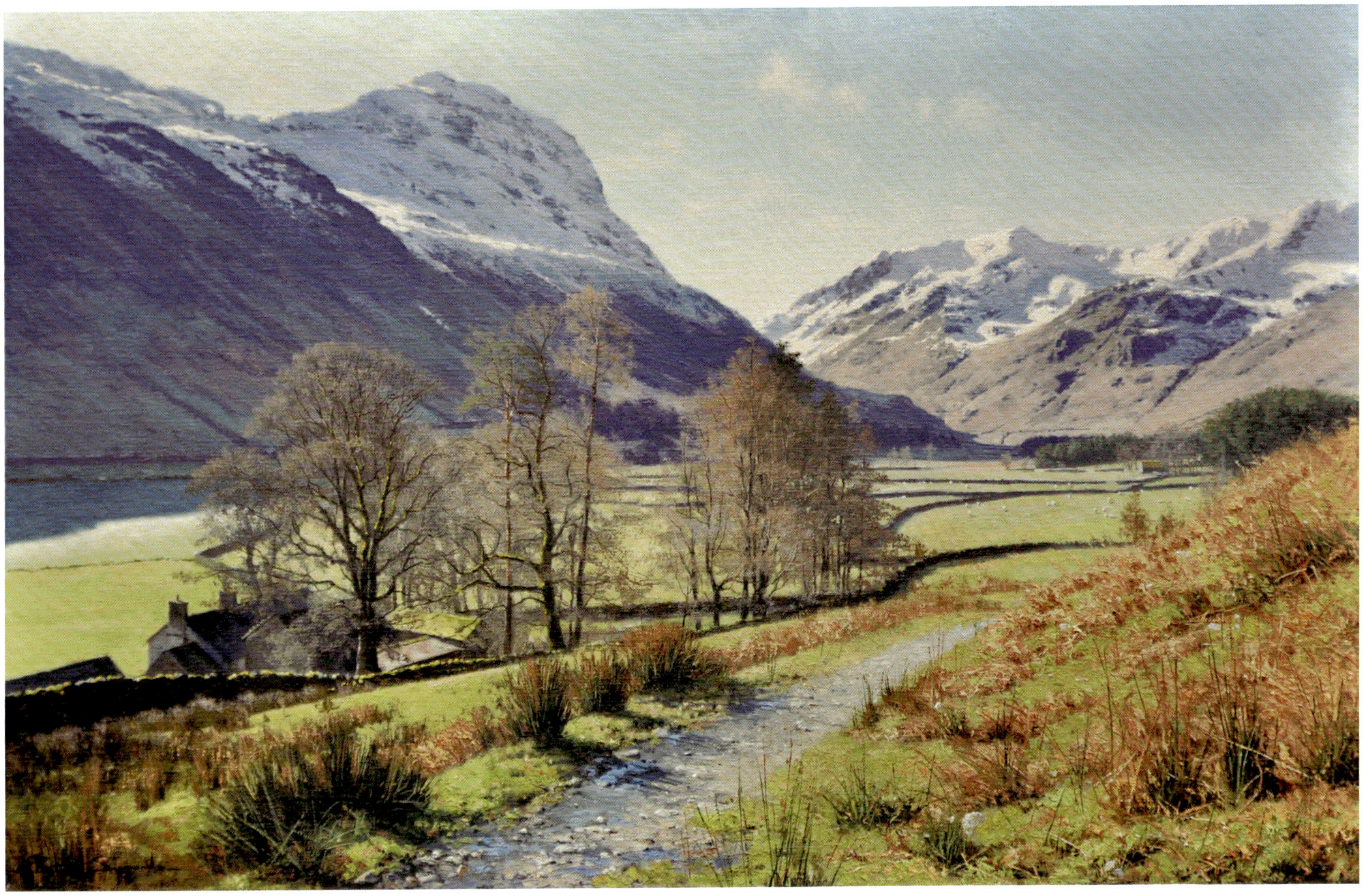

Slaters Bridge, Little Langdale

This picturesque footbridge in Little Langdale is an idyllic place to linger on a sunny day, as the river Brathay which it crosses here flows languidly through some lovely pools on its exit from Little Langdale Tarn a couple of hundred yards away. Half of the narrow little bridge is built up of great slabs of slate laid horizontally over the stone arch, and it was originally constructed for the slaters to reach the quarries around Tilberthwaite and beyond.

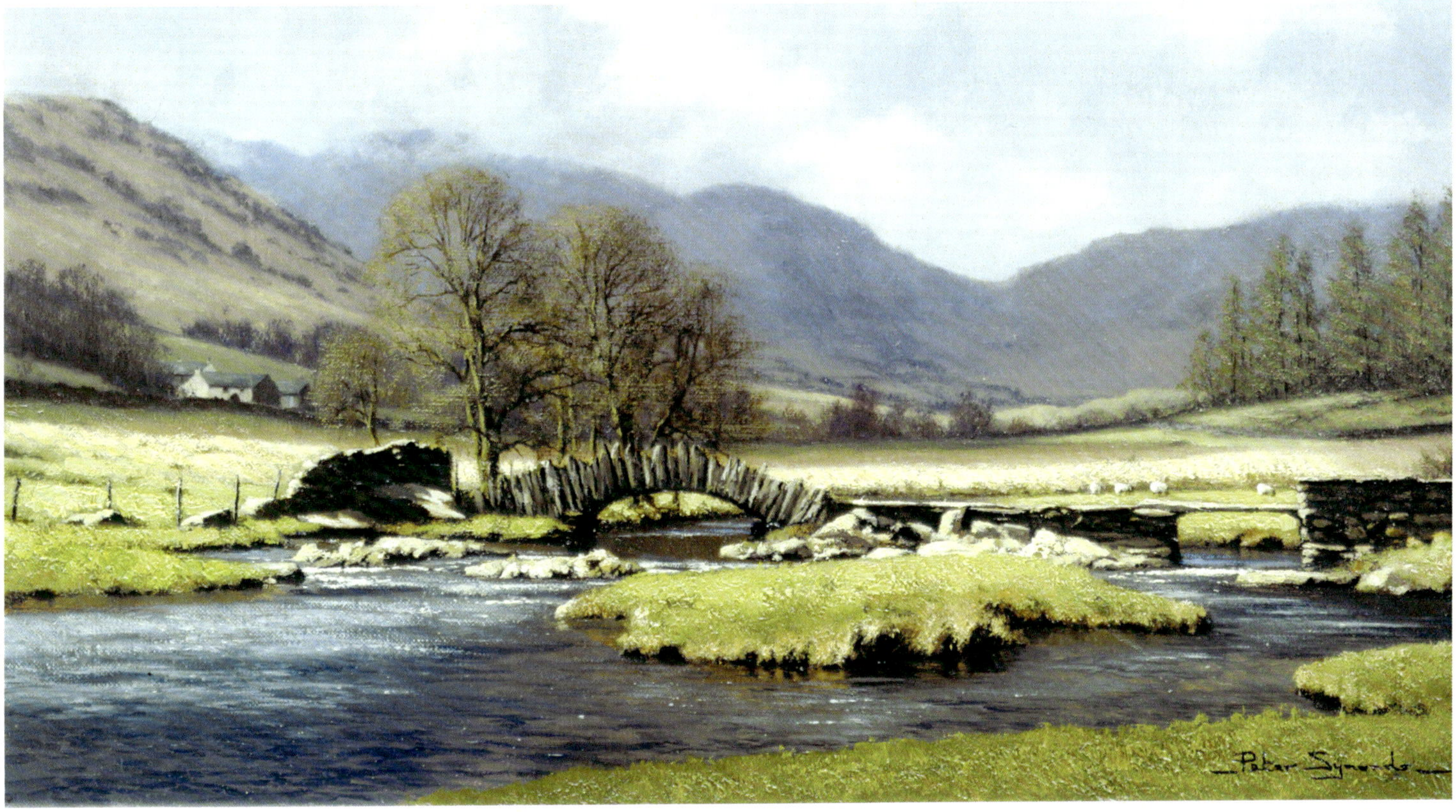
Peter Symonds

Little Langdale Tarn

I particularly like to paint the fells when the atmosphere bathes them in this distant, hazy blue. The colour itself is a joy to paint but it also helps to relieve the monotony of too much greenery.

One of the biggest compositional hurdles when painting from the side of a lake or tarn is knowing what to do with the foreground. There has to be a lead-in to the scene or it can appear very uninteresting. Without the channel between the banks of reeds and grasses this painting would not have worked.

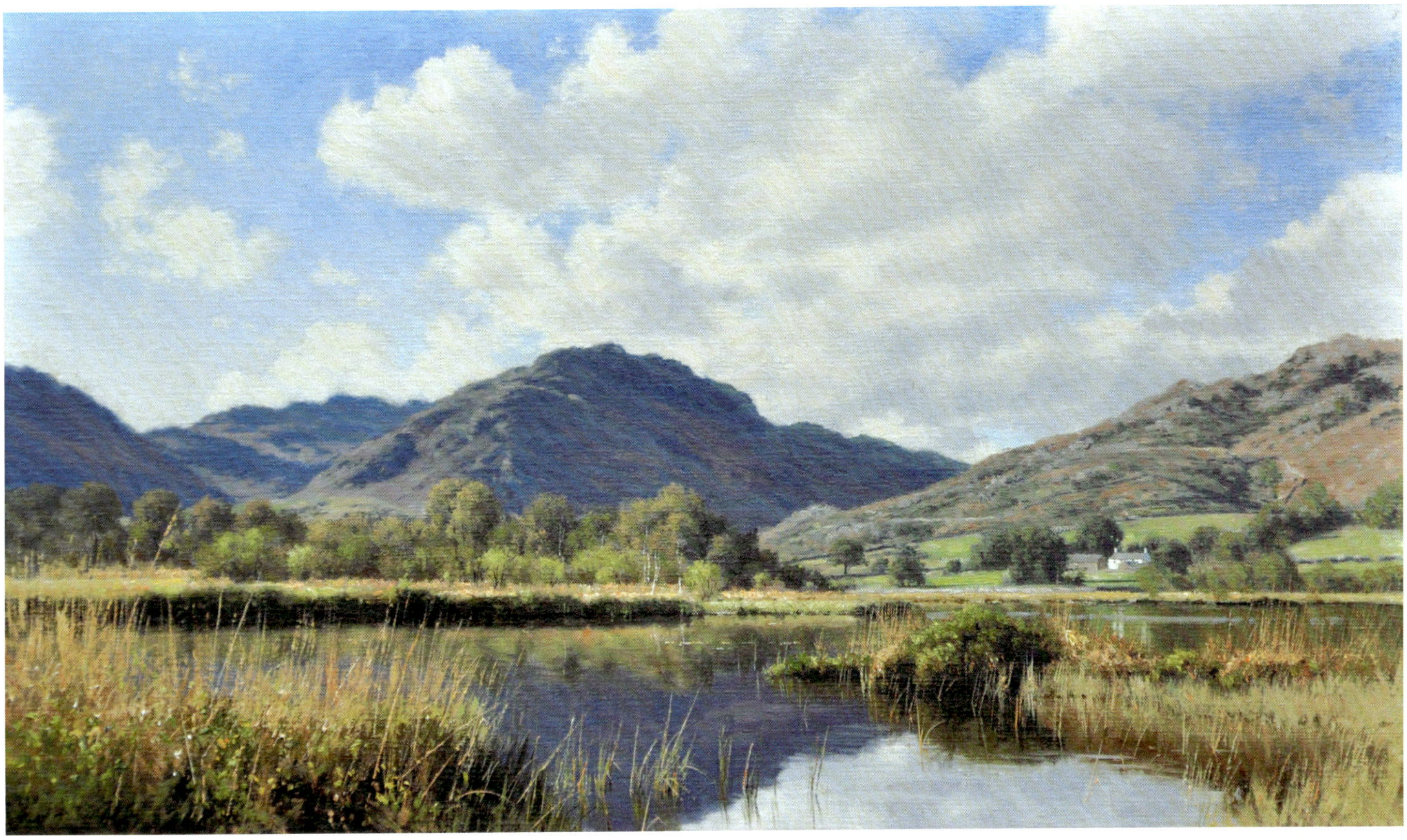

The River Duddon near Ulpha

The River Duddon may lie off the beaten track, but no less an authority than William Wordsworth described it as the most beautiful river that flows from the Lake District's fells. It is a secretive river though, with little public access, despite the fact that a road closely follows its course through most of its journey to the sea.

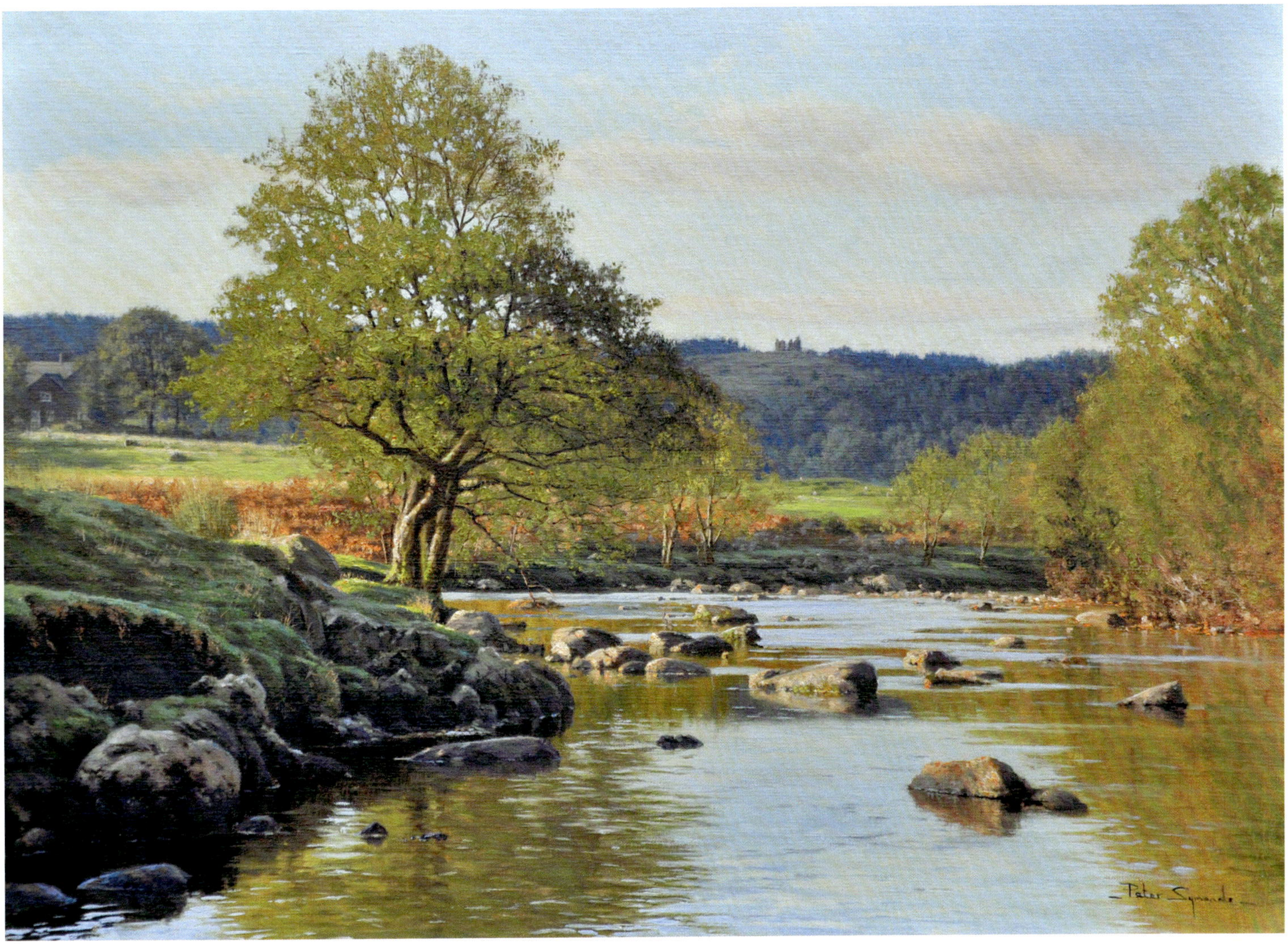

March, Elterwater

In my opinion, the months between October and April are the best times to paint the Lake District, as the range of colours in the landscape are more varied than the all-encompassing greenery that is present in the summer.

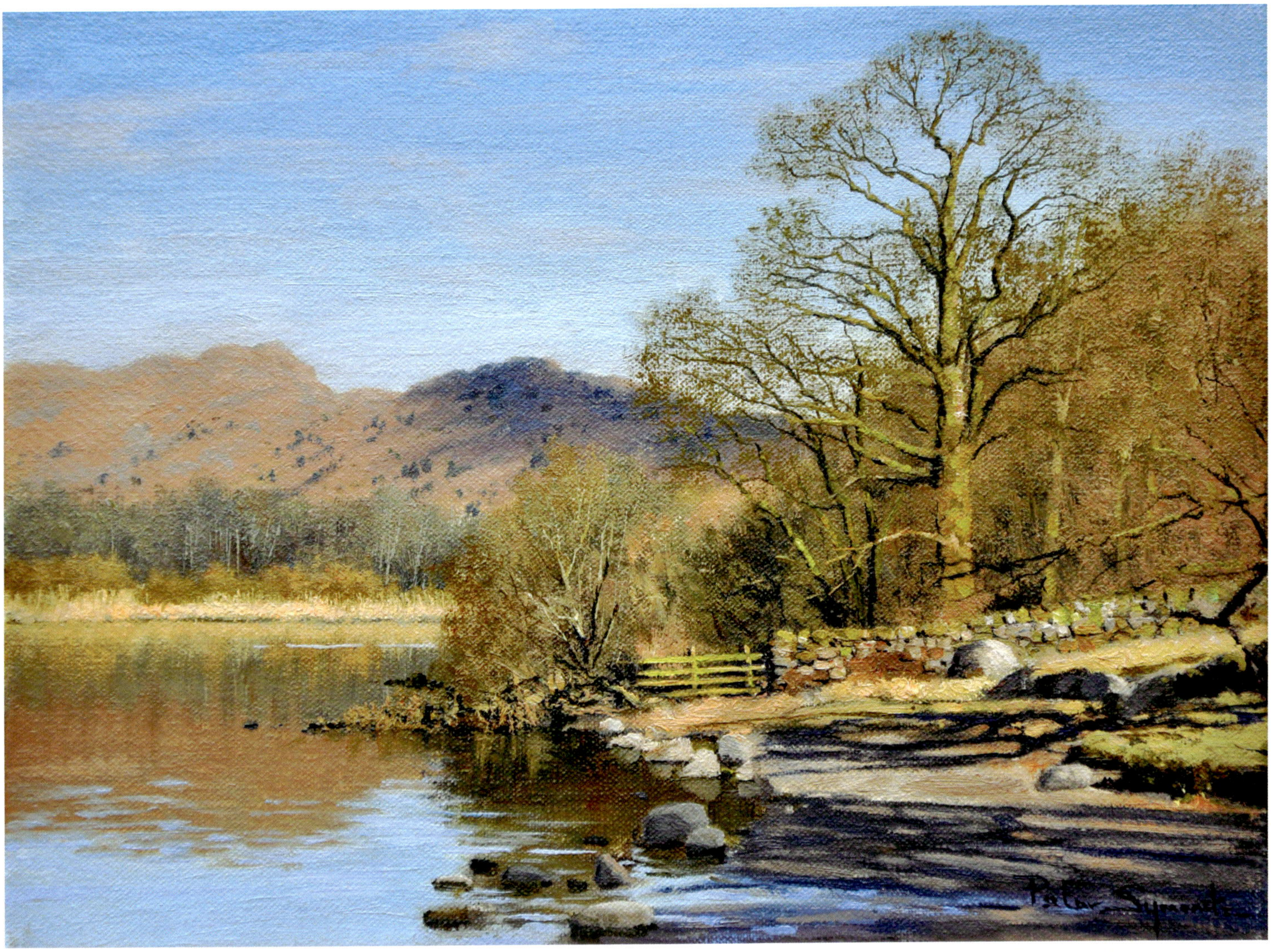

Rosthwaite from the Path to Watendlath

I often have to remind myself that walking in the Lake District is not always about getting to the tops of the fells. When my children were younger one necessarily had to spend far more time on lower paths, such as this one to Watendlath. It is also here on these gentler walks that I still find the greatest inspiration in my never-ending search for subjects to paint.

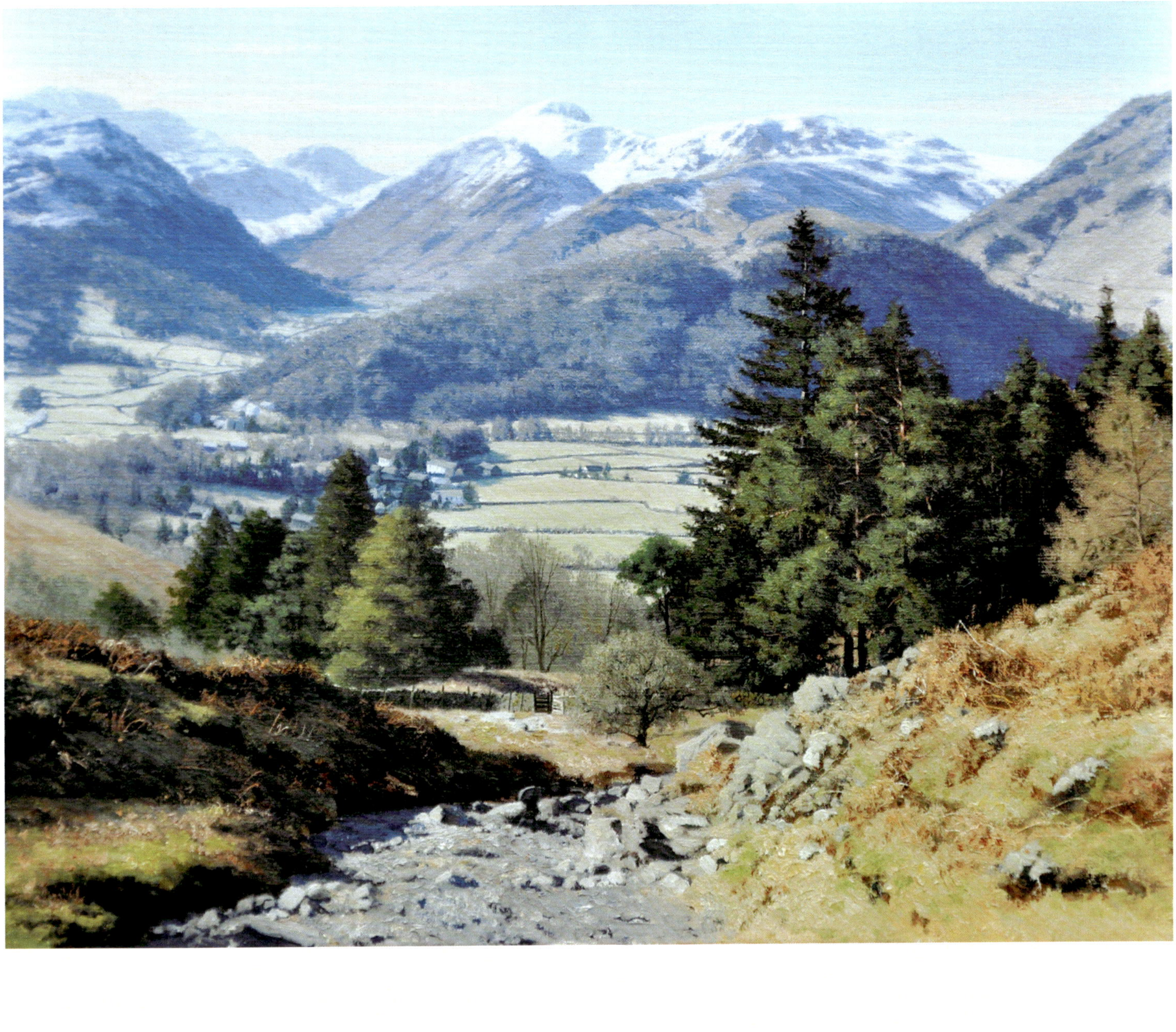

Deepdale

For so many of us, the uncomplicated act of going for a walk is one of life's simplest but richest pleasures. I have been fortunate enough to trek amongst a few of the most breathtaking landscapes in the world in search of subjects to paint. Although it may have something to do with their accessibility, I still find myself spending more time dreaming about the fells and mountains of the Lake District and Scotland than I do of places further afield. So many of us now take our holidays abroad in search of the sun, but I am still amazed that many people who love to walk never go to the north of England or Scotland. The head of Deepdale, for example, though only a few miles from a road, is a great place to visit. It has a wild feel to it, reminiscent of the Scottish glens, and draws me back to it again and again. It also makes a great start for the walks up to Fairfield and St Sunday Crag.

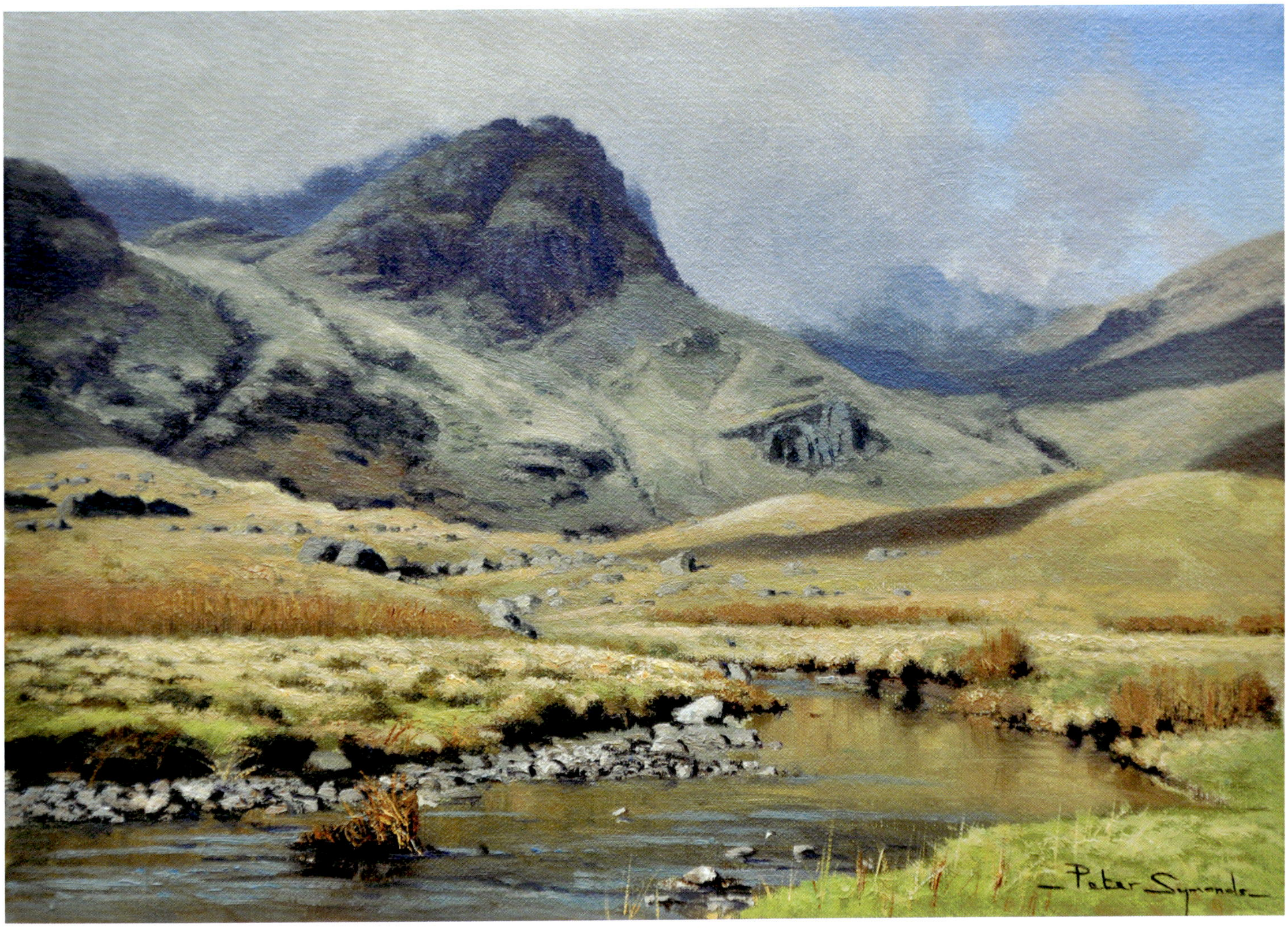
Peter Symonds